ARTHUR & LANCELOT
THE FIGHT FOR CAMELOT

**AN
ENGLISH
LEGEND**

GRAPHIC UNIVERSE™

STORY BY
JEFF LIMKE
PENCILS AND INKS BY
THOMAS YEATES

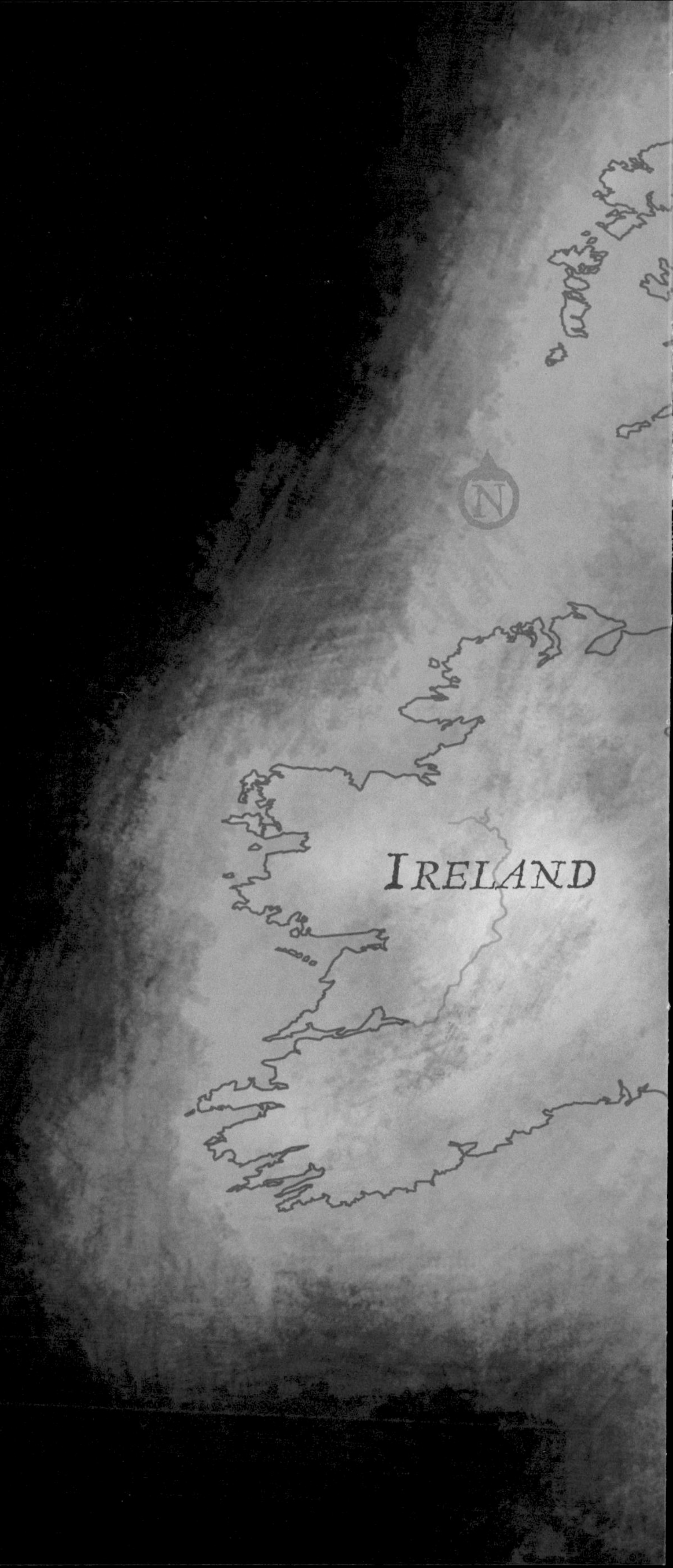
N
IRELAND

ARTHUR & LANCELOT

THE FIGHT FOR CAMELOT

AN ENGLISH LEGEND

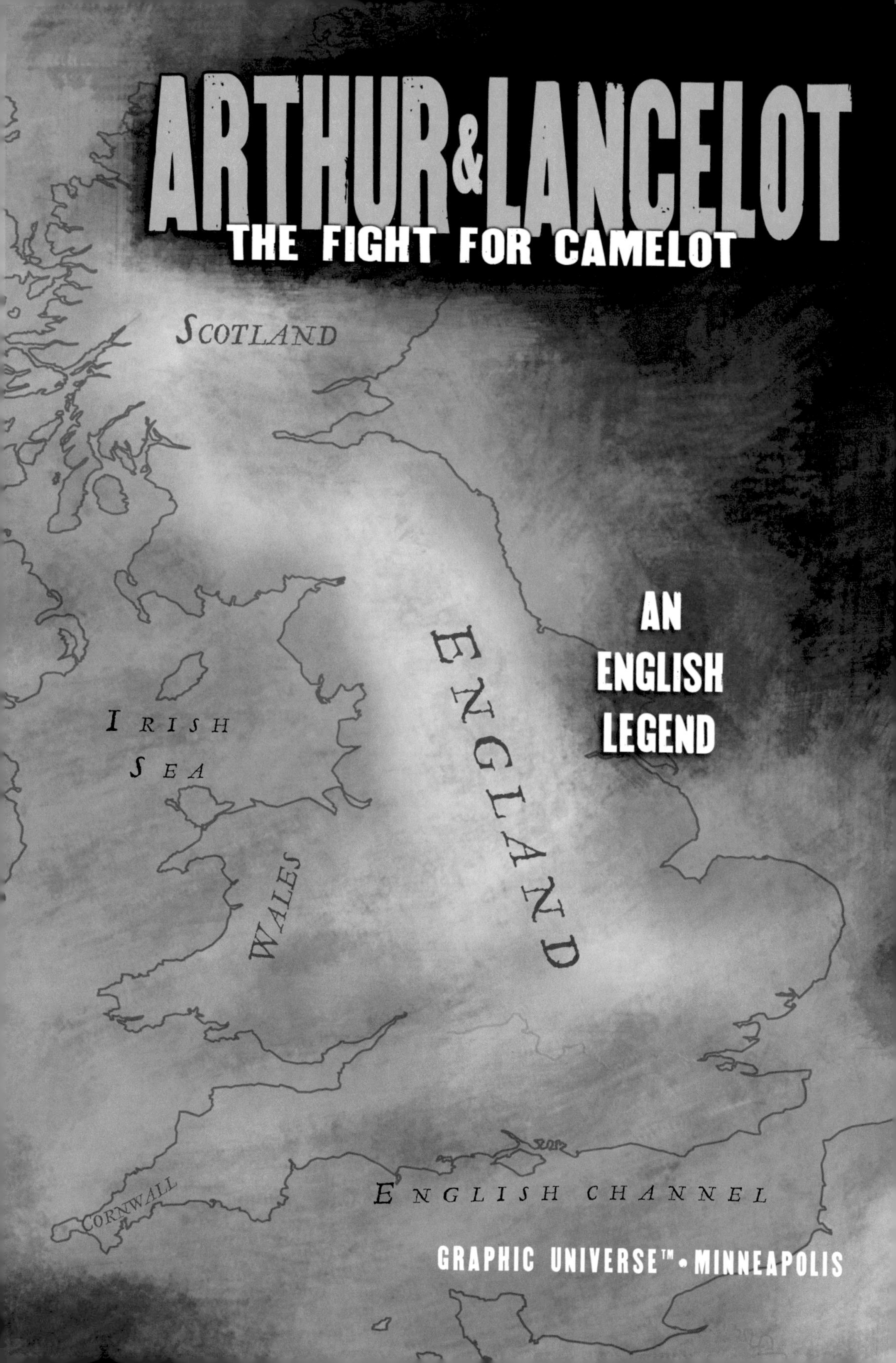

SCOTLAND
IRISH SEA
ENGLAND
WALES
CORNWALL
ENGLISH CHANNEL

GRAPHIC UNIVERSE™ • MINNEAPOLIS

Whether King Arthur was a real person is unknown. But his story is set amid real events in British history. He would have lived around A.D. 400 or 500, when the many small kingdoms of England, Wales, and Cornwall were fighting each other and against foreign invaders. Arthur is thus seen as the king who united and defended early Britain. But often Arthurian tales are depicted as taking place much later in the Middle Ages (about 1100–1300), with knights in armor, jousts, and castles. Arthur & Lancelot: The Fight for Camelot follows that tradition.

As the story begins, Arthur has been king for many years. He rules from Camelot, where a wondrous castle serves as a symbol for the peace of the realm. Arthur leads the Knights of the Round Table, each chosen for his courage and loyalty. But even at Camelot, Arthur must beware those who want to steal his power. As this struggle draws in Arthur's wife, Guinivere, and his friend Lancelot, the king is faced with a conflict between his private feelings and his public duties.

Author Jeff Limke adapted this story from Le Morte d'Arthur, a fifteenth-century collection of Arthurian tales. Artist Thomas Yeates used historical and traditional sources for heraldry, costuming, armor, and other visual details. Consultant Andrew Scheil ensured accuracy.

STORY BY JEFF LIMKE

PENCILS AND INKS BY THOMAS YEATES
WITH SAM GLANZMAN AND KEN HOOPER

COLORING BY HI-FI COLOUR DESIGN

LETTERING BY BRIAN CROWLEY

CONSULTANT: ANDREW SCHEIL, PH.D,
UNIVERSITY OF MINNESOTA

Graphic Universe™
A division of Lerner Publishing Group, Inc.
241 First Avenue North
Minneapolis, MN 55401 U.S.A.

Website address: www.lernerbooks.com

Library of Congress Cataloging-in-Publication Data

Limke, Jeff.
    Arthur and Lancelot : the fight for Camelot / adapted by Jeff Limke from Sir Thomas Malory's Le morte d'Arthur ; illustrations by Thomas Yeates.
    p.   cm. — (Graphic myths and legends)
    Includes index.
    ISBN 978-0-8225-6296-2 (lib. bdg. : alk. paper)
    1. Graphic novels. 2. Arthur, King—Comic books, strips, etc. 3. Lancelot (Legendary character) — Comic books, strips, etc. I. Yeates, Thomas. II. Malory, Thomas, Sir, 15th cent. Morte d'Arthur. III. Title.
PN6727.L53A78 2008
741.5'352—dc22   2006101621

Manufactured in the United States of America
1 2 3 4 5 6 - JR - 13 12 10 09 08

TABLE OF CONTENTS

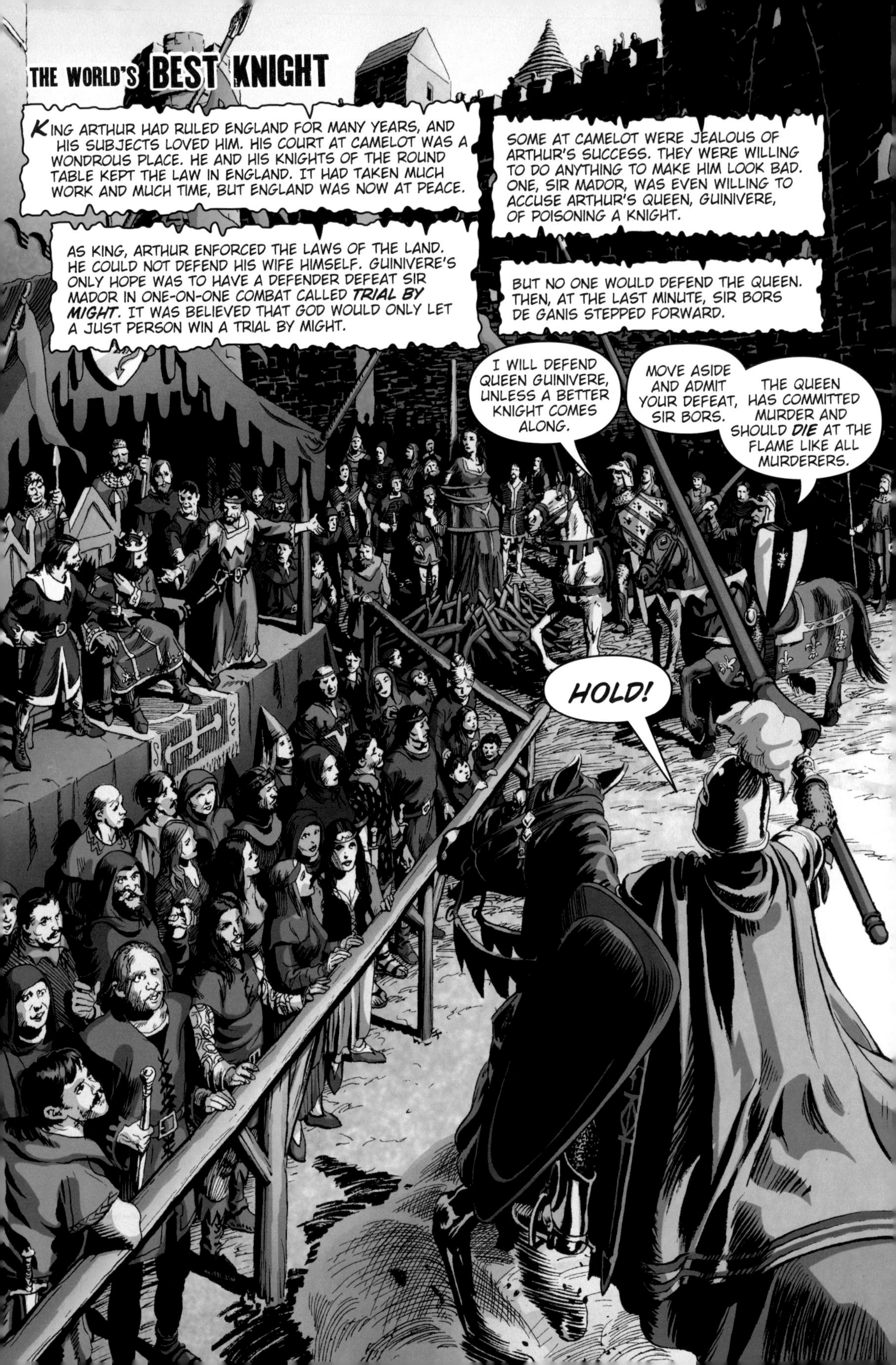
THE WORLD'S BEST KNIGHT
KING ARTHUR HAD RULED ENGLAND FOR MANY YEARS, AND HIS SUBJECTS LOVED HIM. HIS COURT AT CAMELOT WAS A WONDROUS PLACE. HE AND HIS KNIGHTS OF THE ROUND TABLE KEPT THE LAW IN ENGLAND. IT HAD TAKEN MUCH WORK AND MUCH TIME, BUT ENGLAND WAS NOW AT PEACE.
SOME AT CAMELOT WERE JEALOUS OF ARTHUR'S SUCCESS. THEY WERE WILLING TO DO ANYTHING TO MAKE HIM LOOK BAD. ONE, SIR MADOR, WAS EVEN WILLING TO ACCUSE ARTHUR'S QUEEN, GUINIVERE, OF POISONING A KNIGHT.
AS KING, ARTHUR ENFORCED THE LAWS OF THE LAND. HE COULD NOT DEFEND HIS WIFE HIMSELF. GUINIVERE'S ONLY HOPE WAS TO HAVE A DEFENDER DEFEAT SIR MADOR IN ONE-ON-ONE COMBAT CALLED TRIAL BY MIGHT. IT WAS BELIEVED THAT GOD WOULD ONLY LET A JUST PERSON WIN A TRIAL BY MIGHT.
BUT NO ONE WOULD DEFEND THE QUEEN. THEN, AT THE LAST MINUTE, SIR BORS DE GANIS STEPPED FORWARD.
I WILL DEFEND QUEEN GUINIVERE, UNLESS A BETTER KNIGHT COMES ALONG.
MOVE ASIDE AND ADMIT YOUR DEFEAT, SIR BORS.
THE QUEEN HAS COMMITTED MURDER AND SHOULD DIE AT THE FLAME LIKE ALL MURDERERS.
HOLD!

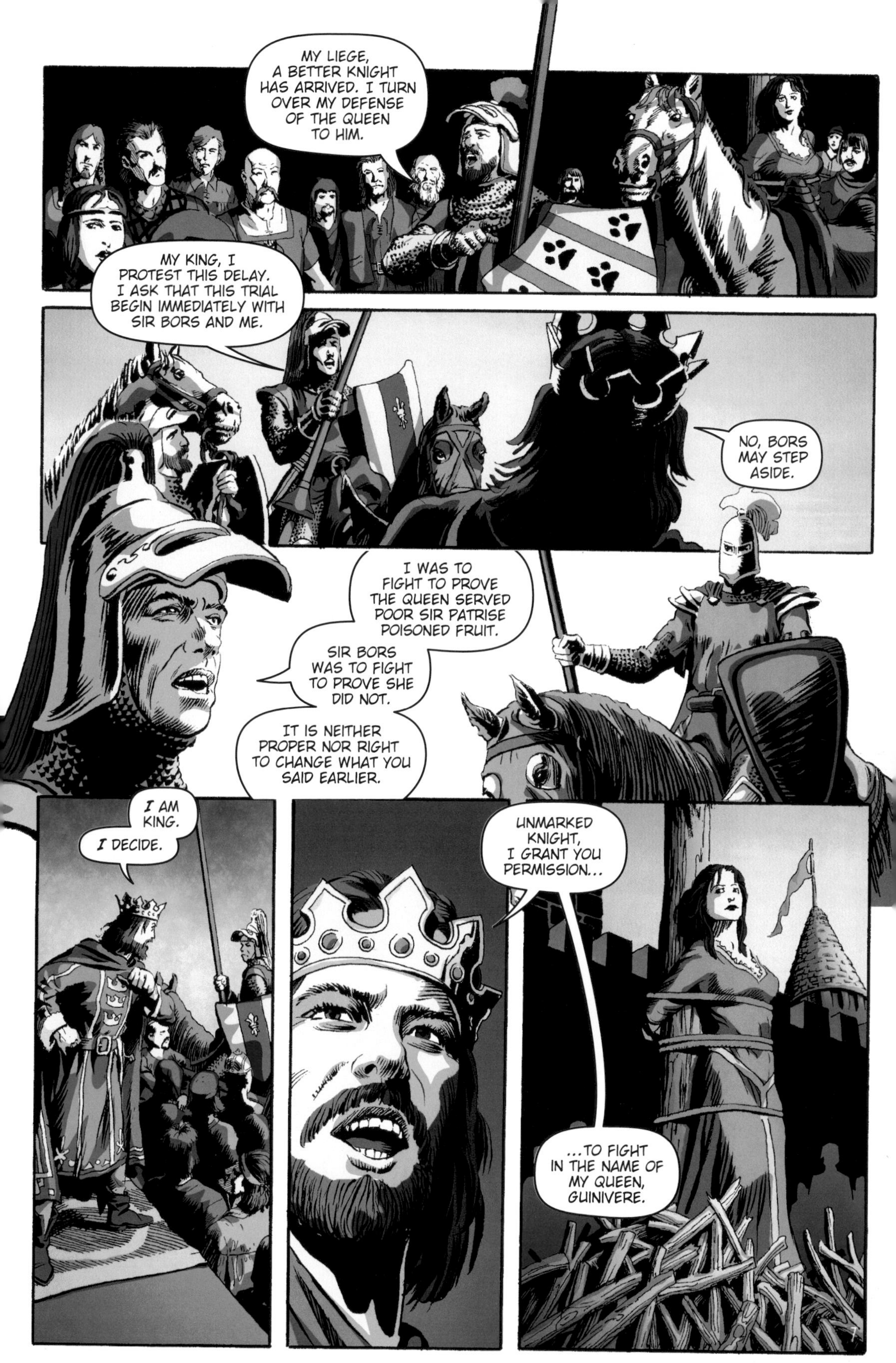

MY LIEGE, A BETTER KNIGHT HAS ARRIVED. I TURN OVER MY DEFENSE OF THE QUEEN TO HIM.
MY KING, I PROTEST THIS DELAY. I ASK THAT THIS TRIAL BEGIN IMMEDIATELY WITH SIR BORS AND ME.
NO, BORS MAY STEP ASIDE.
I WAS TO FIGHT TO PROVE THE QUEEN SERVED POOR SIR PATRISE POISONED FRUIT.
SIR BORS WAS TO FIGHT TO PROVE SHE DID NOT.
IT IS NEITHER PROPER NOR RIGHT TO CHANGE WHAT YOU SAID EARLIER.
I AM KING. I DECIDE.
UNMARKED KNIGHT, I GRANT YOU PERMISSION...
...TO FIGHT IN THE NAME OF MY QUEEN, GUINIVERE.

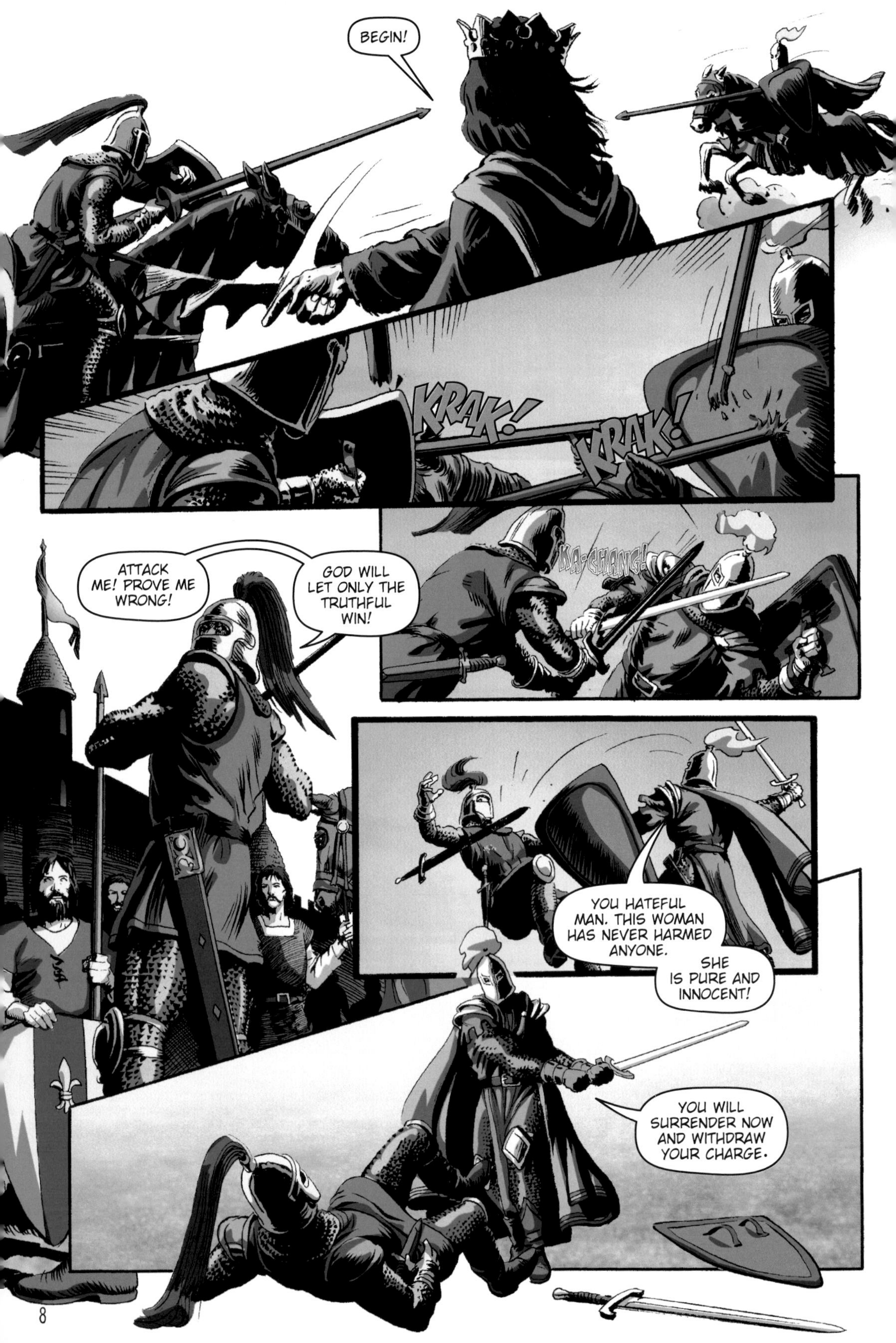
BEGIN!
KRAK!
KRAK!
KA-CHANG!
ATTACK ME! PROVE ME WRONG!
GOD WILL LET ONLY THE TRUTHFUL WIN!
YOU HATEFUL MAN. THIS WOMAN HAS NEVER HARMED ANYONE.
SHE IS PURE AND INNOCENT!
YOU WILL SURRENDER NOW AND WITHDRAW YOUR CHARGE.

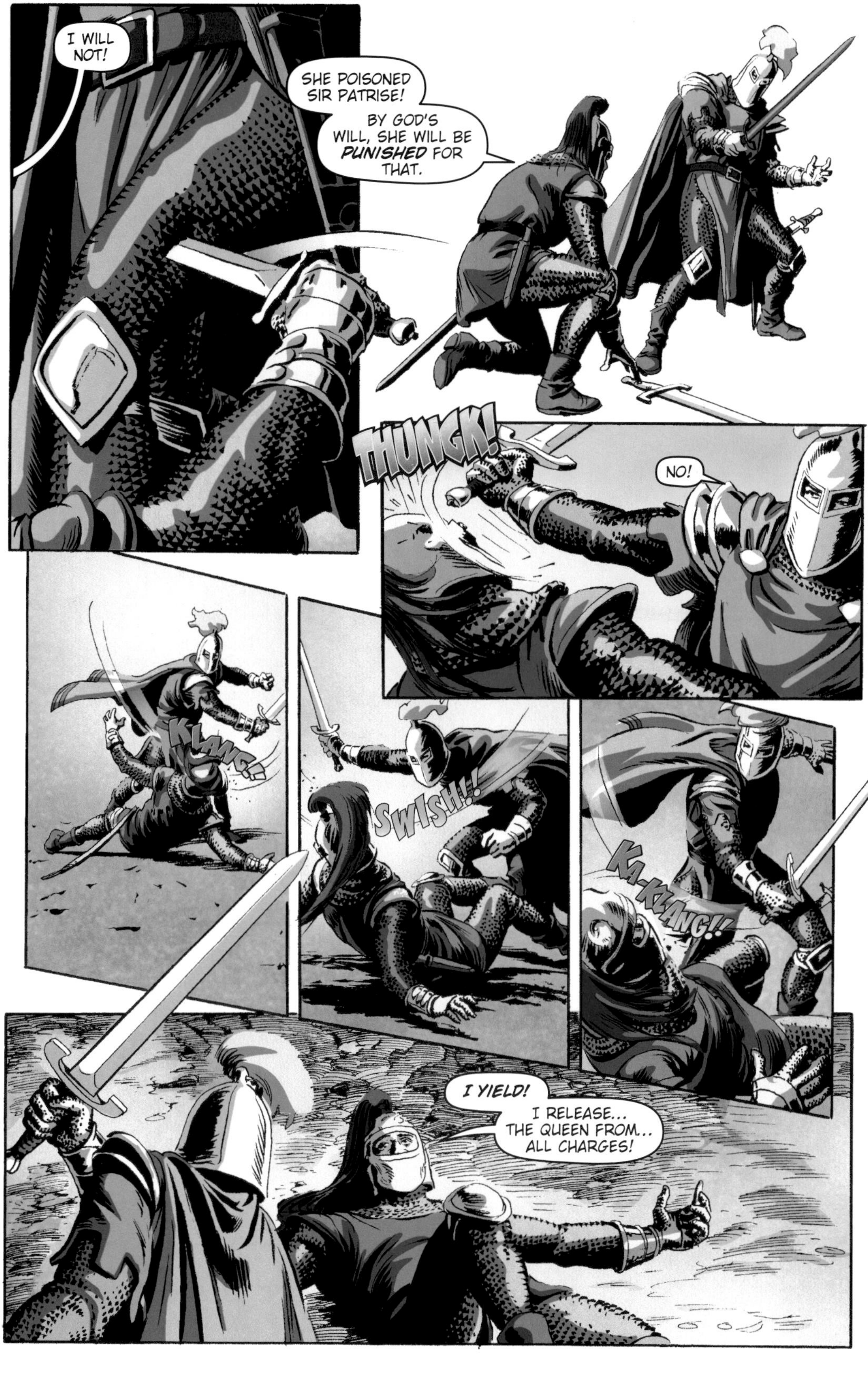
I WILL NOT!
SHE POISONED SIR PATRISE!
BY GOD'S WILL, SHE WILL BE PUNISHED FOR THAT.
THUNGK!
NO!
KLANG!!
SWISH!!
KA-KLANG!!
I YIELD!
I RELEASE... THE QUEEN FROM... ALL CHARGES!

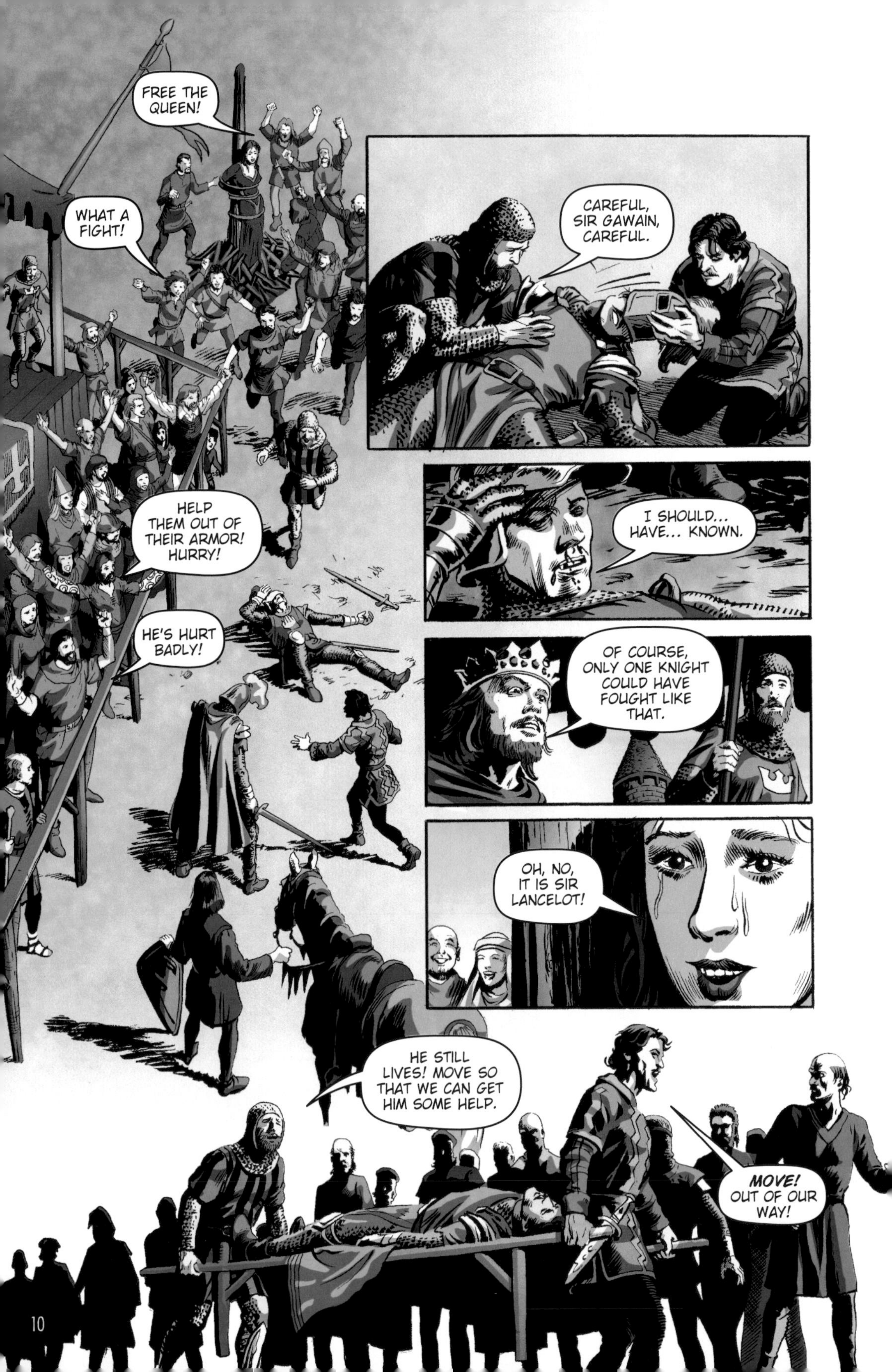
FREE THE QUEEN!
WHAT A FIGHT!
HELP THEM OUT OF THEIR ARMOR! HURRY!
HE'S HURT BADLY!
CAREFUL, SIR GAWAIN, CAREFUL.
I SHOULD... HAVE... KNOWN.
OF COURSE, ONLY ONE KNIGHT COULD HAVE FOUGHT LIKE THAT.
OH, NO, IT IS SIR LANCELOT!
HE STILL LIVES! MOVE SO THAT WE CAN GET HIM SOME HELP.
MOVE! OUT OF OUR WAY!

THE WINCHESTER TOURNAMENT

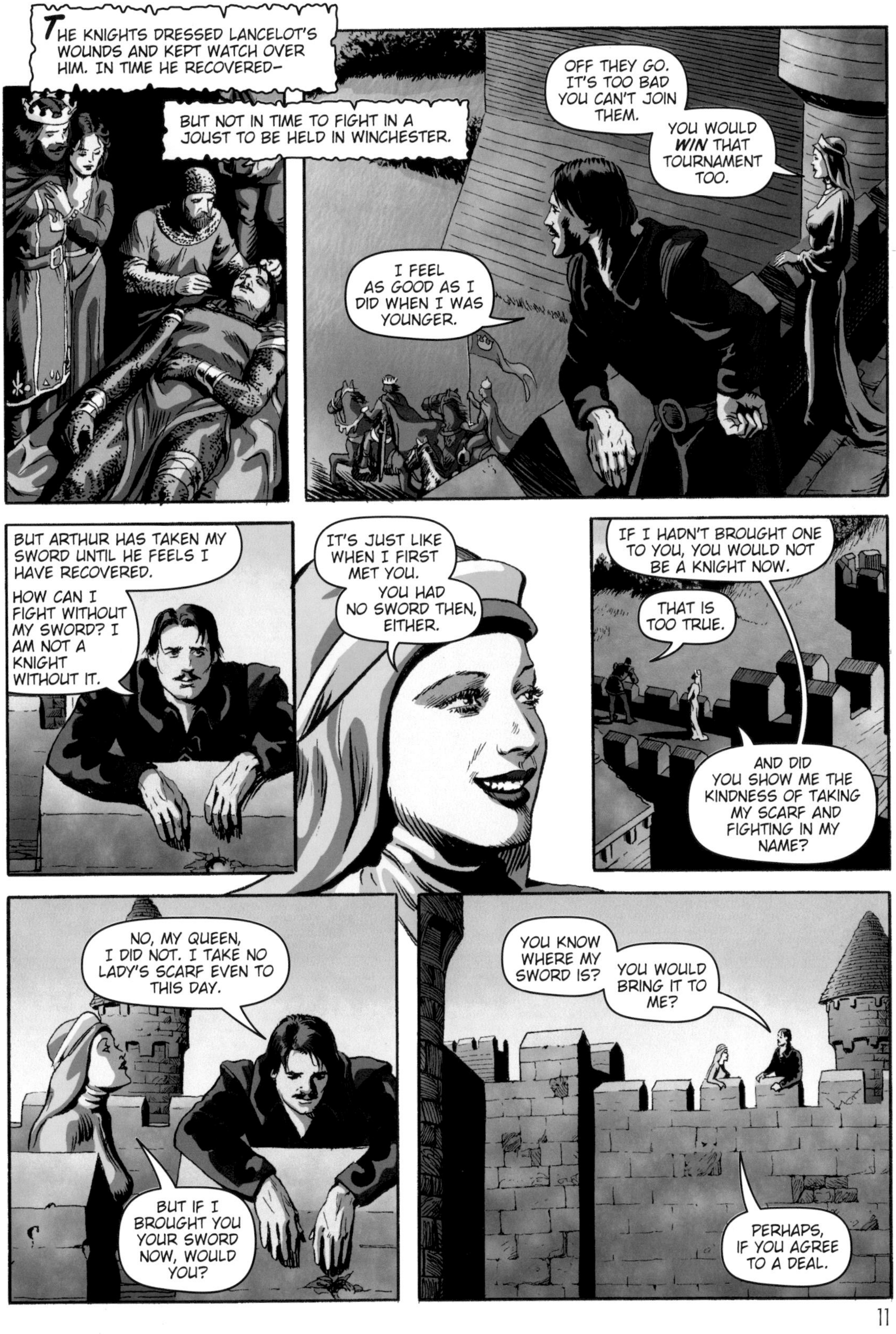

THE KNIGHTS DRESSED LANCELOT'S WOUNDS AND KEPT WATCH OVER HIM. IN TIME HE RECOVERED–
BUT NOT IN TIME TO FIGHT IN A JOUST TO BE HELD IN WINCHESTER.
OFF THEY GO. IT'S TOO BAD YOU CAN'T JOIN THEM.
YOU WOULD WIN THAT TOURNAMENT TOO.
I FEEL AS GOOD AS I DID WHEN I WAS YOUNGER.
BUT ARTHUR HAS TAKEN MY SWORD UNTIL HE FEELS I HAVE RECOVERED.
HOW CAN I FIGHT WITHOUT MY SWORD? I AM NOT A KNIGHT WITHOUT IT.
IT'S JUST LIKE WHEN I FIRST MET YOU.
YOU HAD NO SWORD THEN, EITHER.
IF I HADN'T BROUGHT ONE TO YOU, YOU WOULD NOT BE A KNIGHT NOW.
THAT IS TOO TRUE.
AND DID YOU SHOW ME THE KINDNESS OF TAKING MY SCARF AND FIGHTING IN MY NAME?
NO, MY QUEEN, I DID NOT. I TAKE NO LADY'S SCARF EVEN TO THIS DAY.
BUT IF I BROUGHT YOU YOUR SWORD NOW, WOULD YOU?
YOU KNOW WHERE MY SWORD IS?
YOU WOULD BRING IT TO ME?
PERHAPS, IF YOU AGREE TO A DEAL.

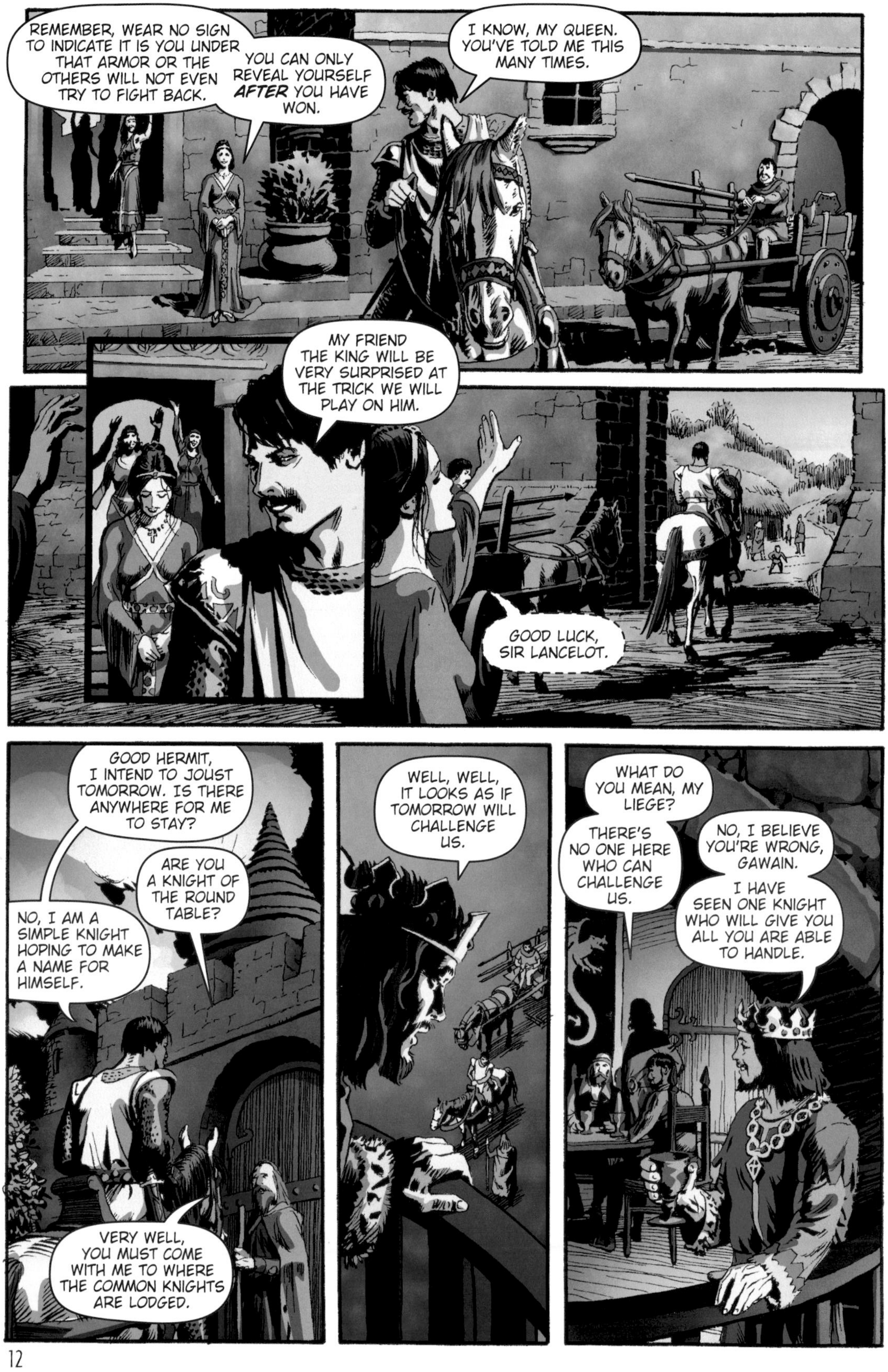
REMEMBER, WEAR NO SIGN TO INDICATE IT IS YOU UNDER THAT ARMOR OR THE OTHERS WILL NOT EVEN TRY TO FIGHT BACK.
YOU CAN ONLY REVEAL YOURSELF *AFTER* YOU HAVE WON.
I KNOW, MY QUEEN. YOU'VE TOLD ME THIS MANY TIMES.
MY FRIEND THE KING WILL BE VERY SURPRISED AT THE TRICK WE WILL PLAY ON HIM.
GOOD LUCK, SIR LANCELOT.
GOOD HERMIT, I INTEND TO JOUST TOMORROW. IS THERE ANYWHERE FOR ME TO STAY?
ARE YOU A KNIGHT OF THE ROUND TABLE?
NO, I AM A SIMPLE KNIGHT HOPING TO MAKE A NAME FOR HIMSELF.
VERY WELL, YOU MUST COME WITH ME TO WHERE THE COMMON KNIGHTS ARE LODGED.
WELL, WELL, IT LOOKS AS IF TOMORROW WILL CHALLENGE US.
WHAT DO YOU MEAN, MY LIEGE?
THERE'S NO ONE HERE WHO CAN CHALLENGE US.
NO, I BELIEVE YOU'RE WRONG, GAWAIN.
I HAVE SEEN ONE KNIGHT WHO WILL GIVE YOU ALL YOU ARE ABLE TO HANDLE.

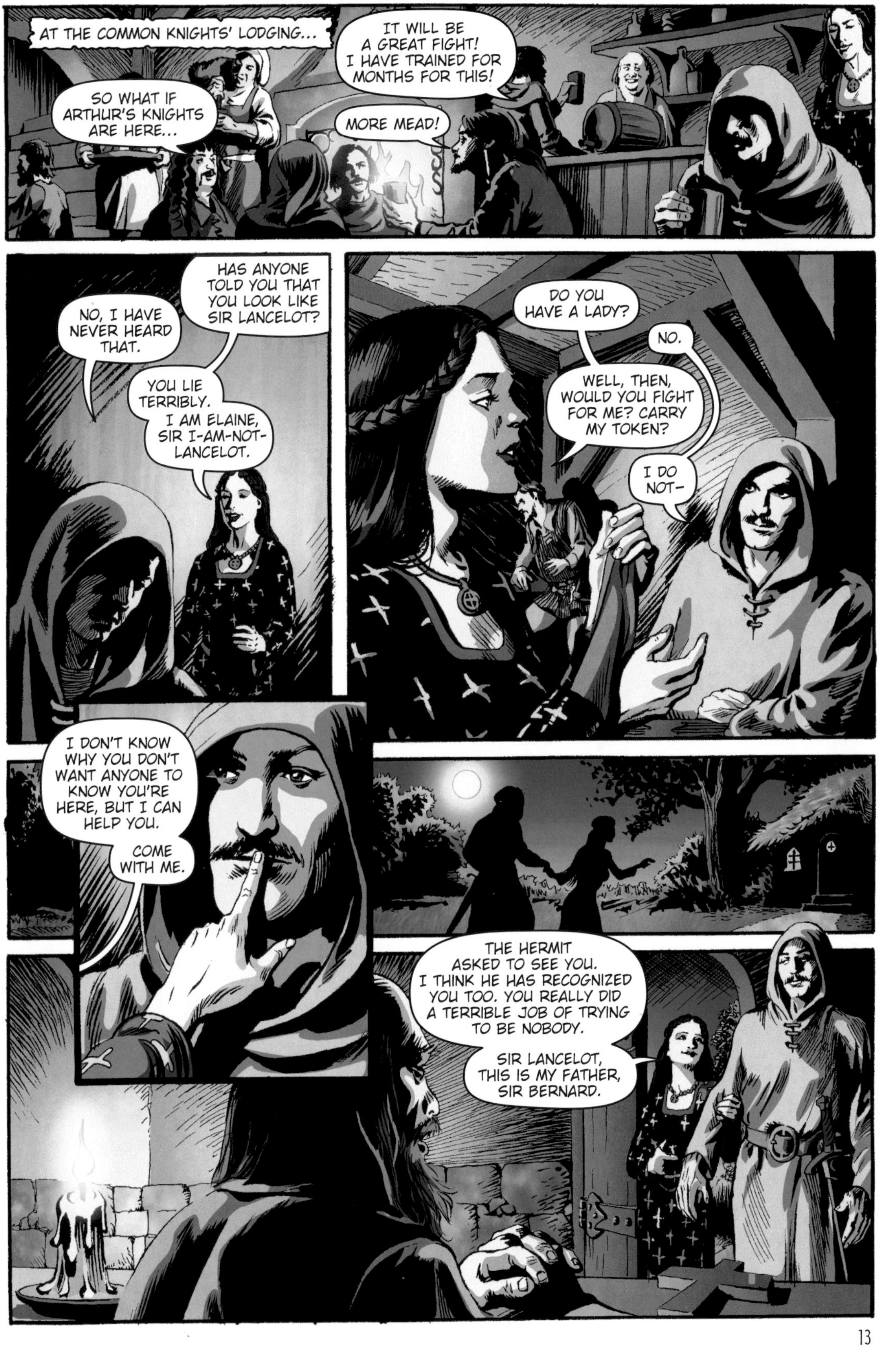
AT THE COMMON KNIGHTS' LODGING...
SO WHAT IF ARTHUR'S KNIGHTS ARE HERE...
IT WILL BE A GREAT FIGHT! I HAVE TRAINED FOR MONTHS FOR THIS!
MORE MEAD!
HAS ANYONE TOLD YOU THAT YOU LOOK LIKE SIR LANCELOT?
NO, I HAVE NEVER HEARD THAT.
YOU LIE TERRIBLY.
I AM ELAINE, SIR I-AM-NOT-LANCELOT.
DO YOU HAVE A LADY?
NO.
WELL, THEN, WOULD YOU FIGHT FOR ME? CARRY MY TOKEN?
I DO NOT-
I DON'T KNOW WHY YOU DON'T WANT ANYONE TO KNOW YOU'RE HERE, BUT I CAN HELP YOU.
COME WITH ME.
THE HERMIT ASKED TO SEE YOU. I THINK HE HAS RECOGNIZED YOU TOO. YOU REALLY DID A TERRIBLE JOB OF TRYING TO BE NOBODY.
SIR LANCELOT, THIS IS MY FATHER, SIR BERNARD.

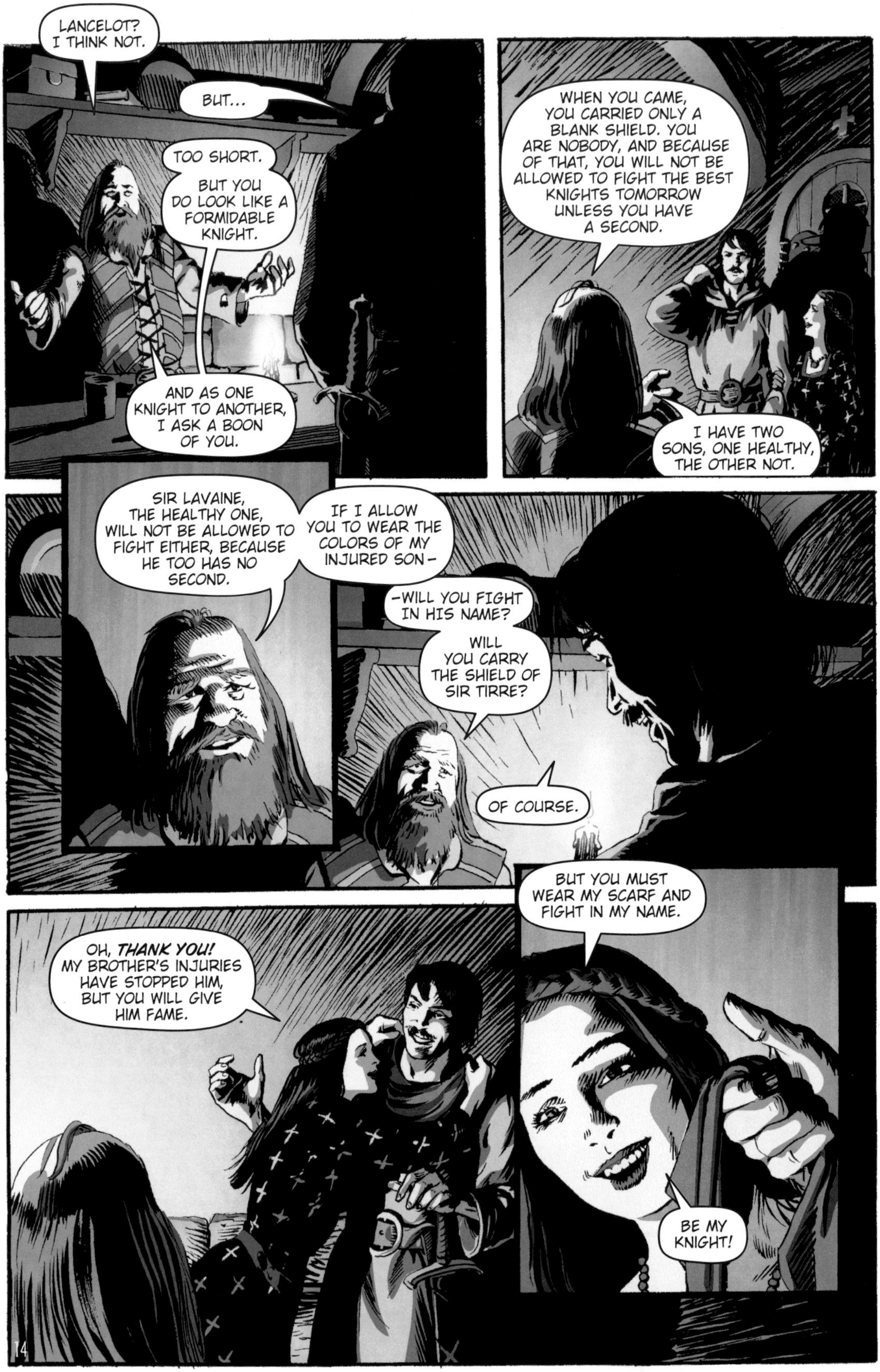
LANCELOT? I THINK NOT.
BUT...
TOO SHORT.
BUT YOU DO LOOK LIKE A FORMIDABLE KNIGHT.
AND AS ONE KNIGHT TO ANOTHER, I ASK A BOON OF YOU.
WHEN YOU CAME, YOU CARRIED ONLY A BLANK SHIELD. YOU ARE NOBODY, AND BECAUSE OF THAT, YOU WILL NOT BE ALLOWED TO FIGHT THE BEST KNIGHTS TOMORROW UNLESS YOU HAVE A SECOND.
I HAVE TWO SONS, ONE HEALTHY, THE OTHER NOT.
SIR LAVAINE, THE HEALTHY ONE, WILL NOT BE ALLOWED TO FIGHT EITHER, BECAUSE HE TOO HAS NO SECOND.
IF I ALLOW YOU TO WEAR THE COLORS OF MY INJURED SON–
–WILL YOU FIGHT IN HIS NAME?
WILL YOU CARRY THE SHIELD OF SIR TIRRE?
OF COURSE.
OH, ***THANK YOU!*** MY BROTHER'S INJURIES HAVE STOPPED HIM, BUT YOU WILL GIVE HIM FAME.
BUT YOU MUST WEAR MY SCARF AND FIGHT IN MY NAME.
BE MY KNIGHT!

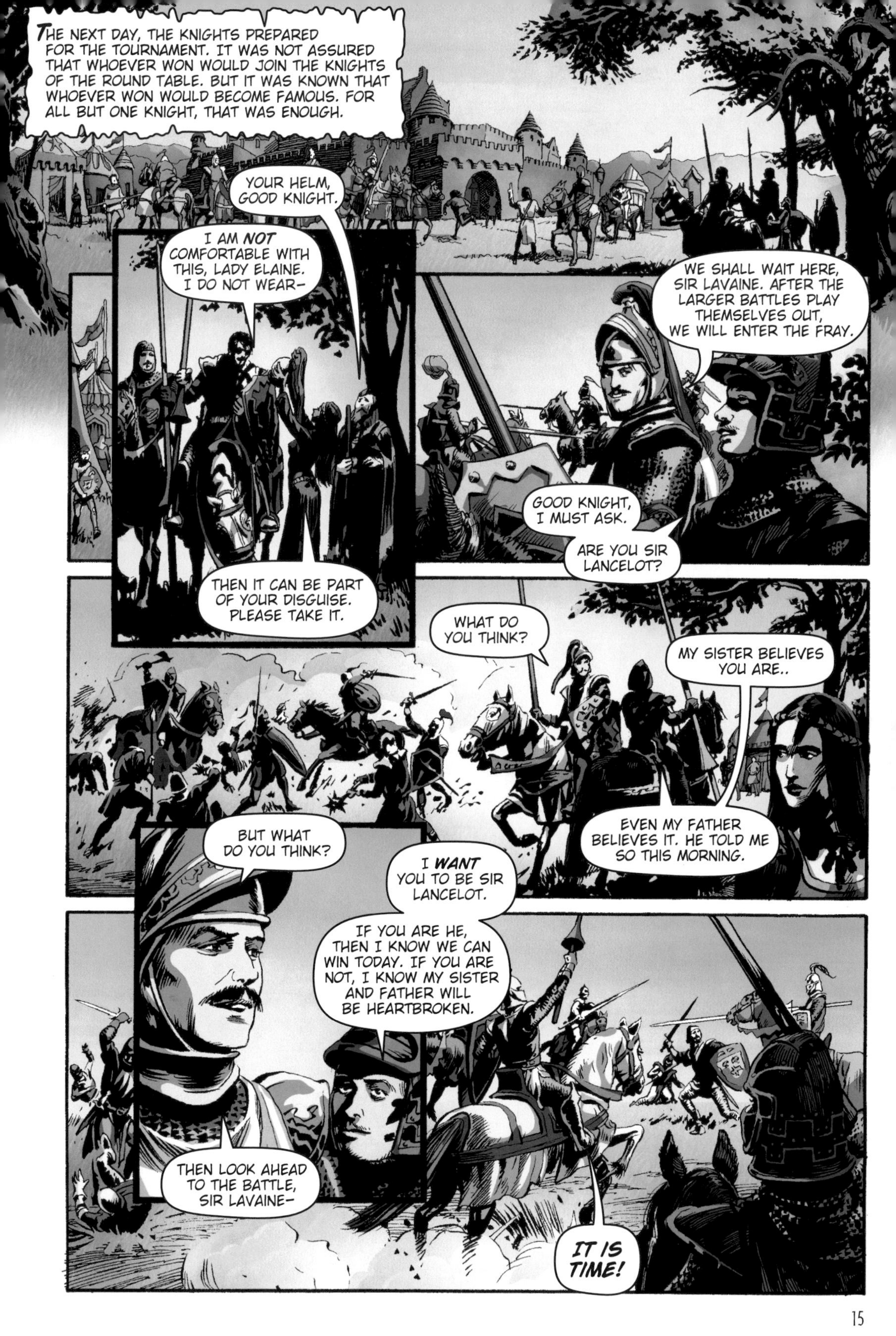

THE NEXT DAY, THE KNIGHTS PREPARED FOR THE TOURNAMENT. IT WAS NOT ASSURED THAT WHOEVER WON WOULD JOIN THE KNIGHTS OF THE ROUND TABLE. BUT IT WAS KNOWN THAT WHOEVER WON WOULD BECOME FAMOUS. FOR ALL BUT ONE KNIGHT, THAT WAS ENOUGH.
YOUR HELM, GOOD KNIGHT.
I AM NOT COMFORTABLE WITH THIS, LADY ELAINE. I DO NOT WEAR–
THEN IT CAN BE PART OF YOUR DISGUISE. PLEASE TAKE IT.
WE SHALL WAIT HERE, SIR LAVAINE. AFTER THE LARGER BATTLES PLAY THEMSELVES OUT, WE WILL ENTER THE FRAY.
GOOD KNIGHT, I MUST ASK.
ARE YOU SIR LANCELOT?
WHAT DO YOU THINK?
MY SISTER BELIEVES YOU ARE..
EVEN MY FATHER BELIEVES IT. HE TOLD ME SO THIS MORNING.
BUT WHAT DO YOU THINK?
I WANT YOU TO BE SIR LANCELOT.
IF YOU ARE HE, THEN I KNOW WE CAN WIN TODAY. IF YOU ARE NOT, I KNOW MY SISTER AND FATHER WILL BE HEARTBROKEN.
THEN LOOK AHEAD TO THE BATTLE, SIR LAVAINE–
IT IS TIME!

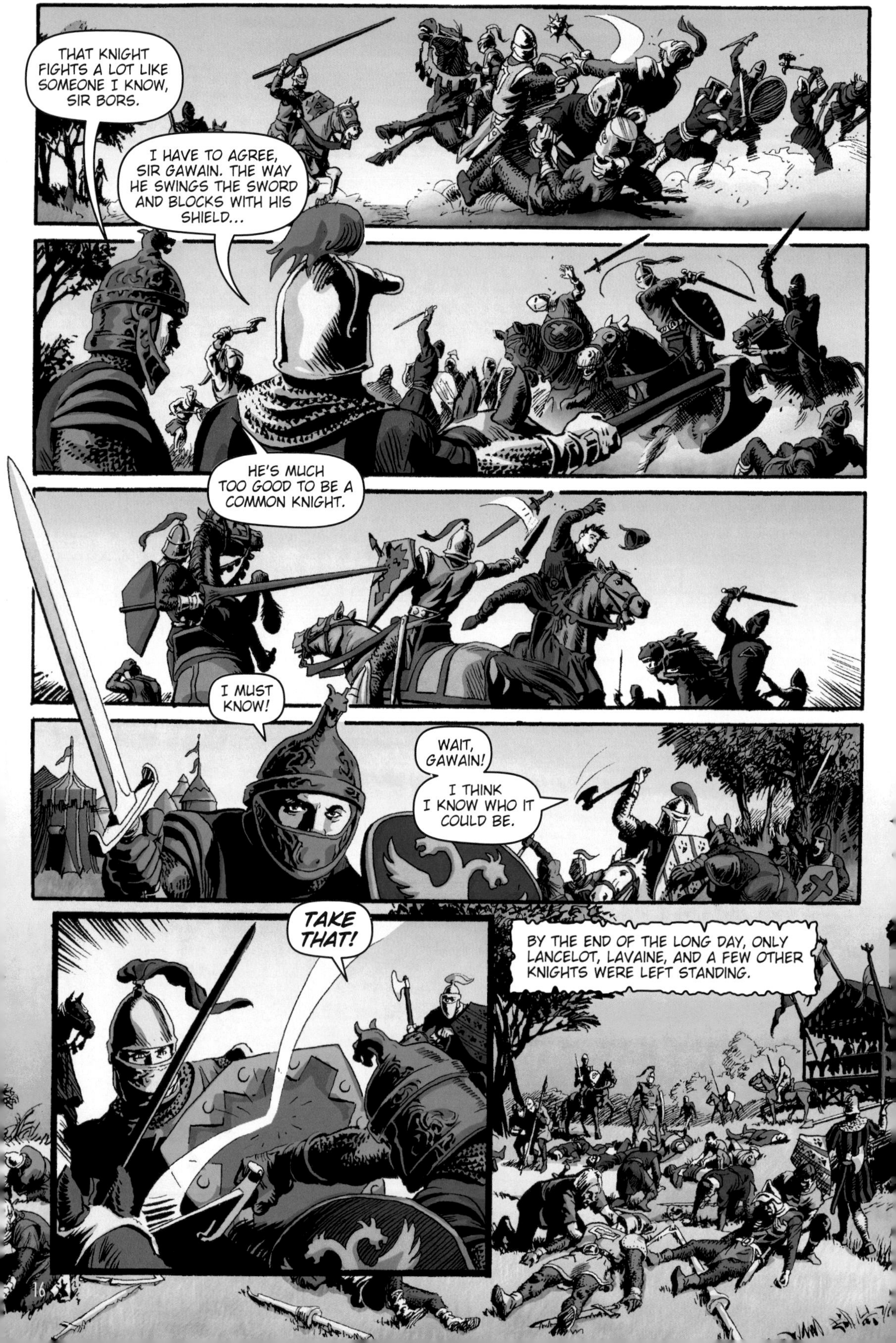
THAT KNIGHT FIGHTS A LOT LIKE SOMEONE I KNOW, SIR BORS.
I HAVE TO AGREE, SIR GAWAIN. THE WAY HE SWINGS THE SWORD AND BLOCKS WITH HIS SHIELD...
HE'S MUCH TOO GOOD TO BE A COMMON KNIGHT.
I MUST KNOW!
WAIT, GAWAIN!
I THINK I KNOW WHO IT COULD BE.
TAKE THAT!
BY THE END OF THE LONG DAY, ONLY LANCELOT, LAVAINE, AND A FEW OTHER KNIGHTS WERE LEFT STANDING.

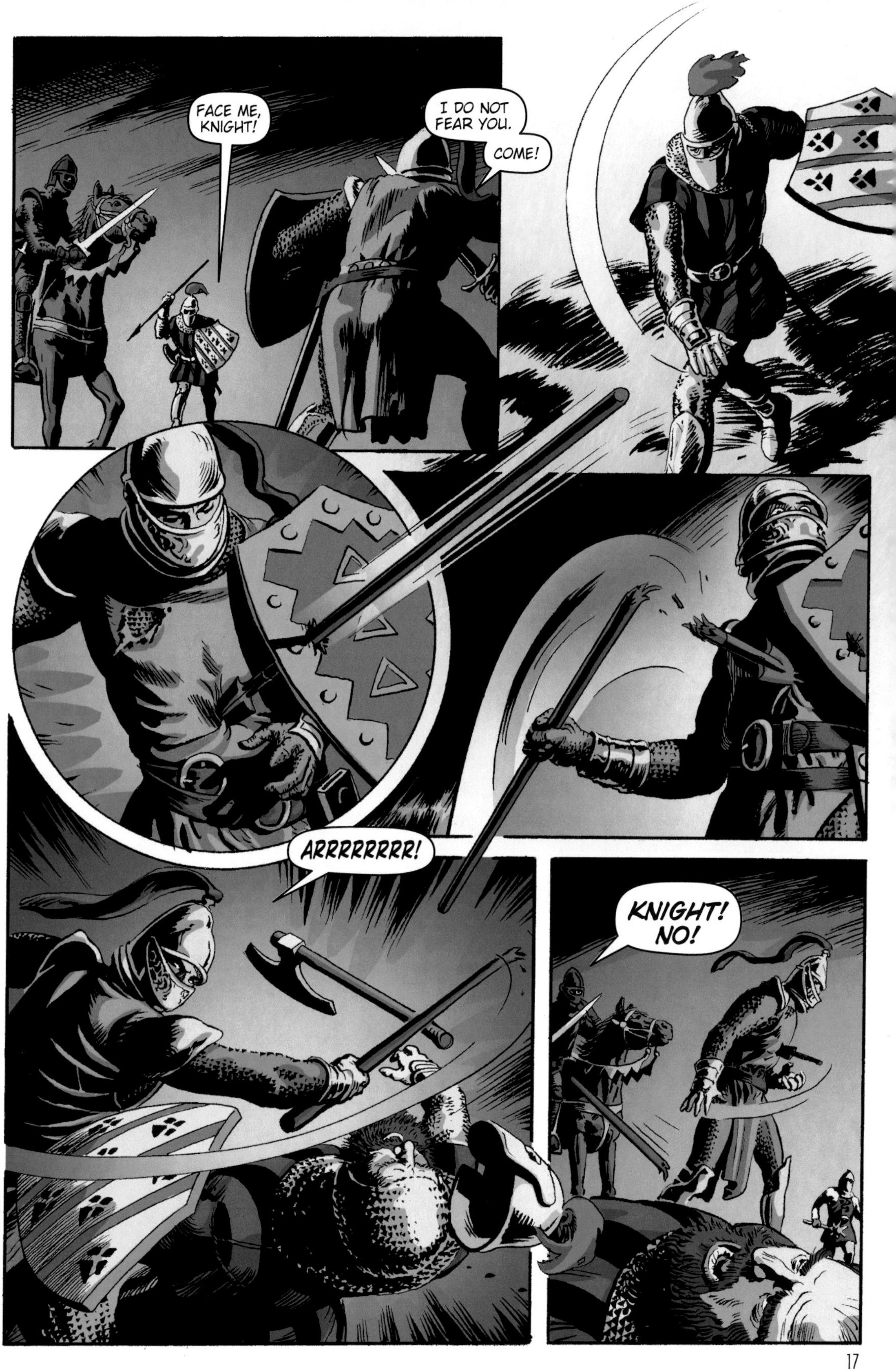
FACE ME, KNIGHT!
I DO NOT FEAR YOU.
COME!
ARRRRRRRR!
KNIGHT! NO!

FOUL SIR MELIGRANCE

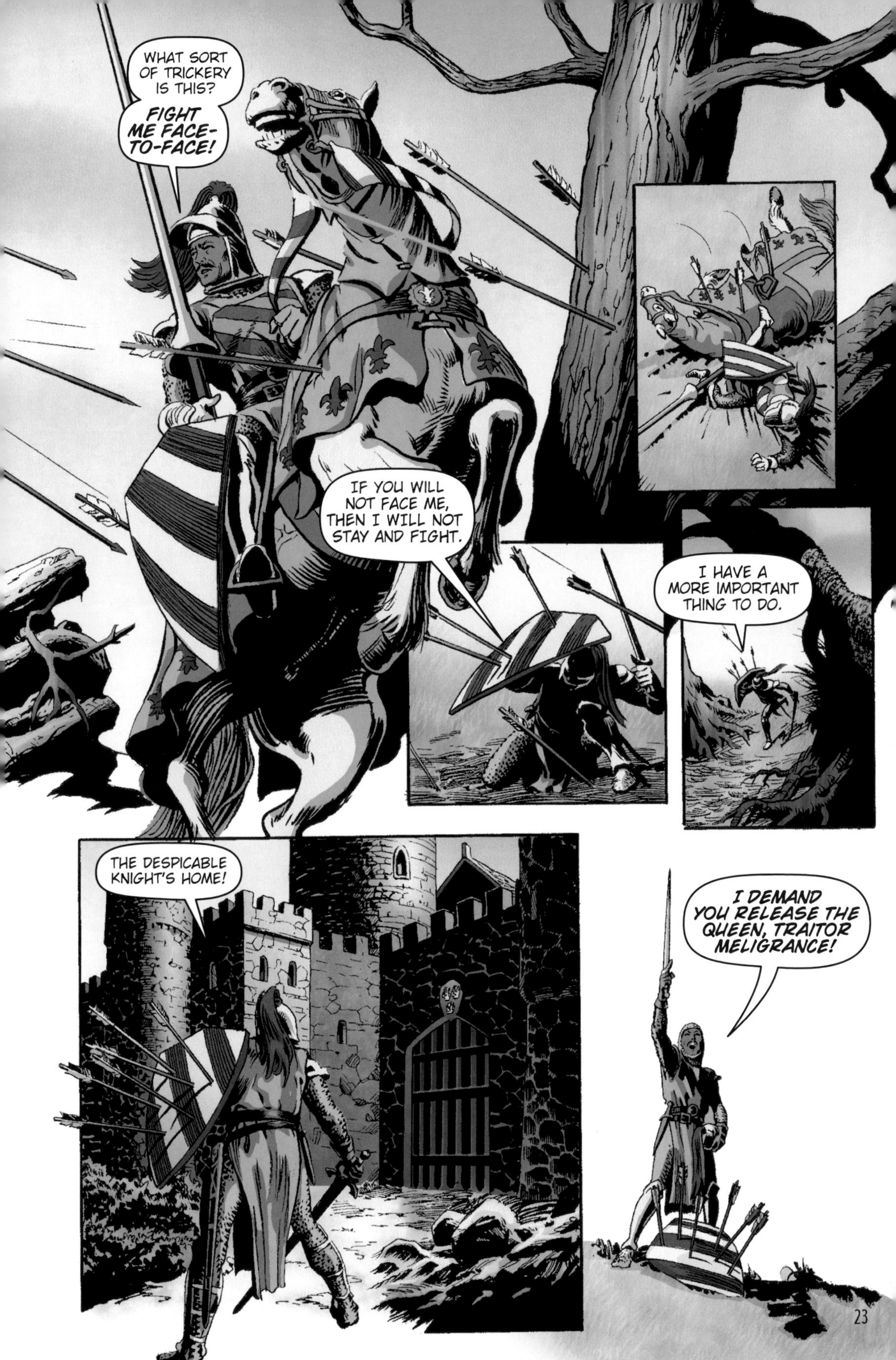
WHAT SORT OF TRICKERY IS THIS?
FIGHT ME FACE-TO-FACE!
IF YOU WILL NOT FACE ME, THEN I WILL NOT STAY AND FIGHT.
I HAVE A MORE IMPORTANT THING TO DO.
THE DESPICABLE KNIGHT'S HOME!
I DEMAND YOU RELEASE THE QUEEN, TRAITOR MELIGRANCE!

24

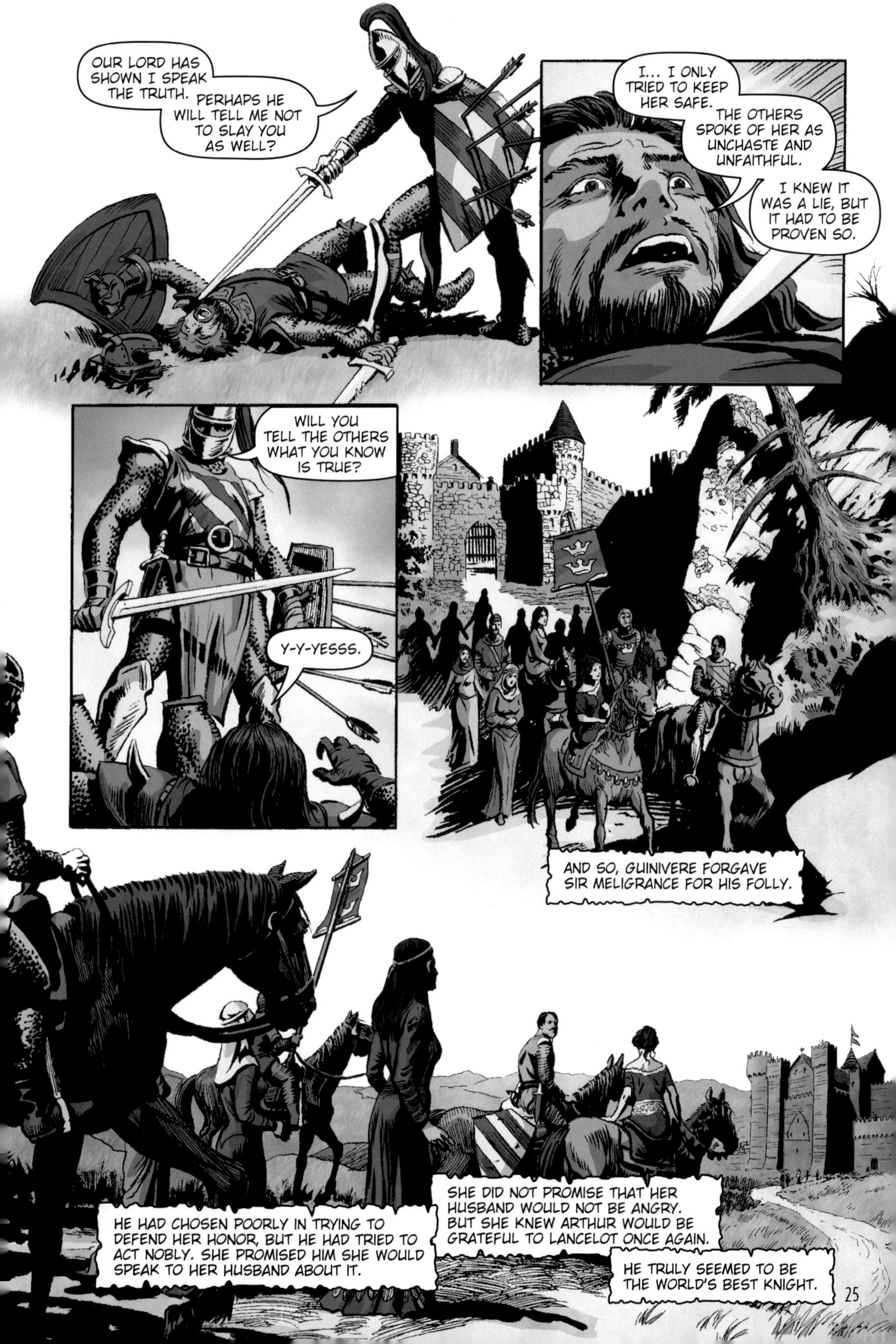
OUR LORD HAS SHOWN I SPEAK THE TRUTH.
PERHAPS HE WILL TELL ME NOT TO SLAY YOU AS WELL?
I... I ONLY TRIED TO KEEP HER SAFE.
THE OTHERS SPOKE OF HER AS UNCHASTE AND UNFAITHFUL.
I KNEW IT WAS A LIE, BUT IT HAD TO BE PROVEN SO.
WILL YOU TELL THE OTHERS WHAT YOU KNOW IS TRUE?
Y-Y-YESSS.
AND SO, GUINIVERE FORGAVE SIR MELIGRANCE FOR HIS FOLLY.
HE HAD CHOSEN POORLY IN TRYING TO DEFEND HER HONOR, BUT HE HAD TRIED TO ACT NOBLY. SHE PROMISED HIM SHE WOULD SPEAK TO HER HUSBAND ABOUT IT.
SHE DID NOT PROMISE THAT HER HUSBAND WOULD NOT BE ANGRY. BUT SHE KNEW ARTHUR WOULD BE GRATEFUL TO LANCELOT ONCE AGAIN.
HE TRULY SEEMED TO BE THE WORLD'S BEST KNIGHT.

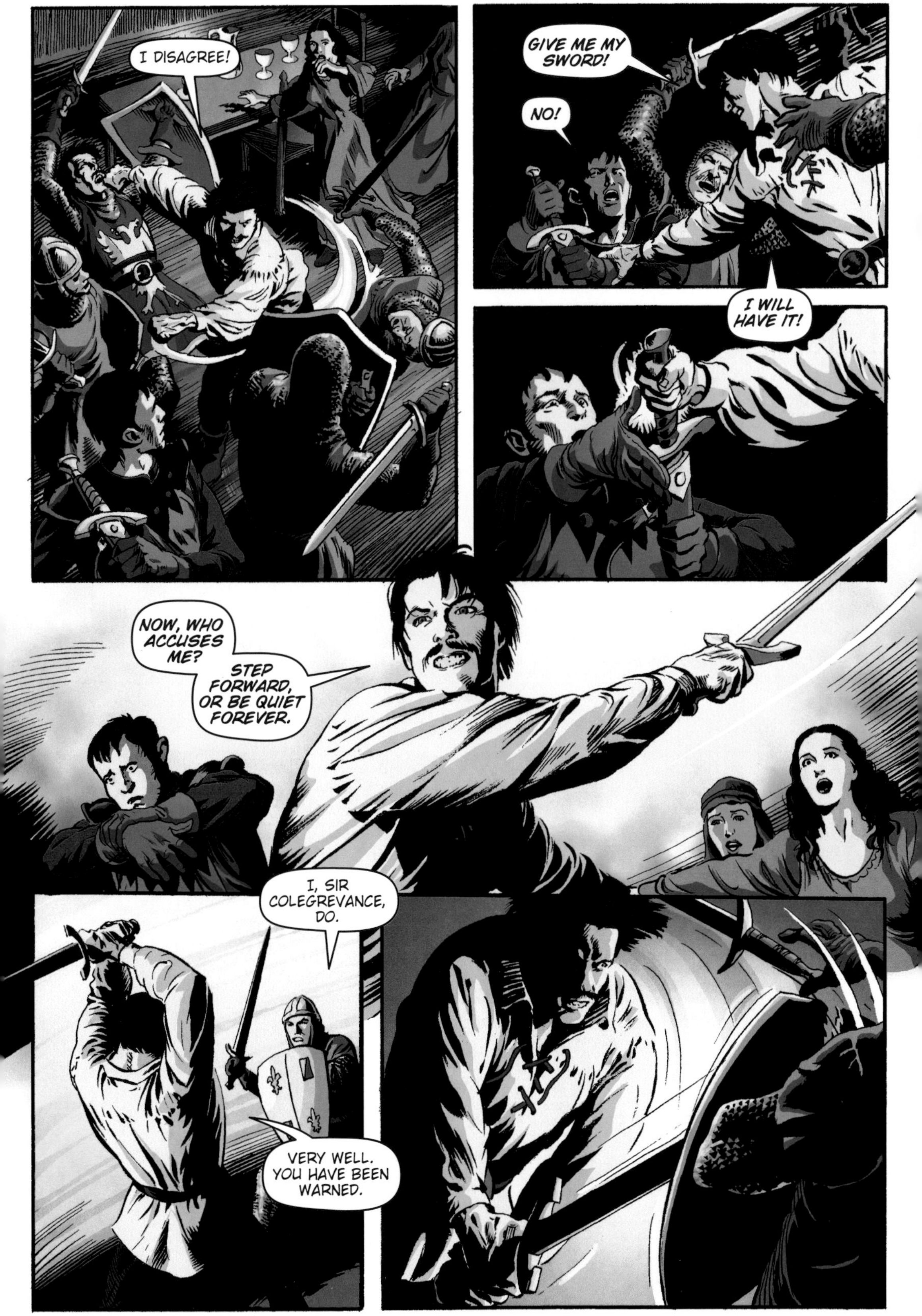
I DISAGREE!
GIVE ME MY SWORD!
NO!
I WILL HAVE IT!
NOW, WHO ACCUSES ME?
STEP FORWARD, OR BE QUIET FOREVER.
I, SIR COLEGREVANCE, DO.
VERY WELL. YOU HAVE BEEN WARNED.

29

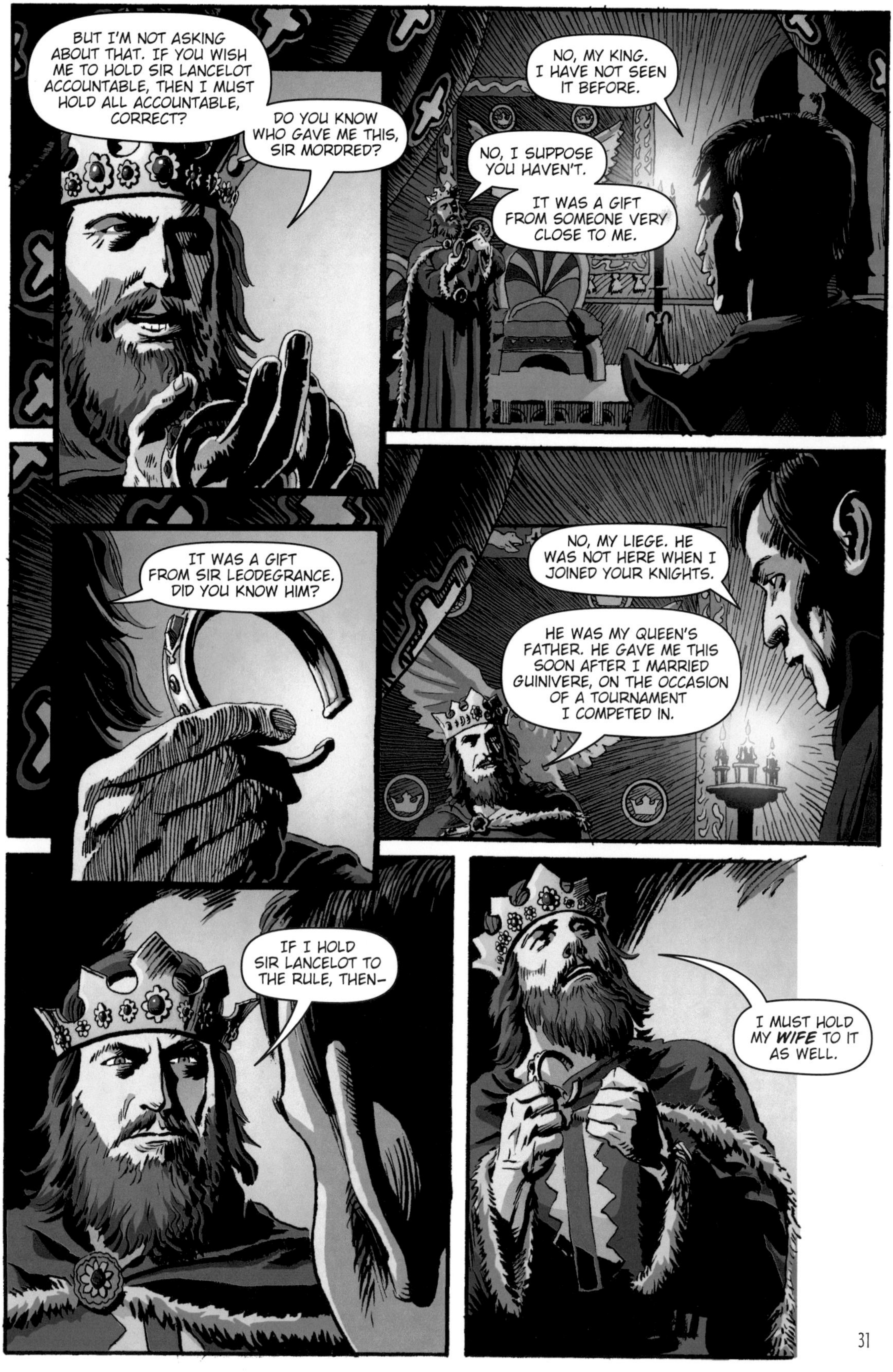
BUT I'M NOT ASKING ABOUT THAT. IF YOU WISH ME TO HOLD SIR LANCELOT ACCOUNTABLE, THEN I MUST HOLD ALL ACCOUNTABLE, CORRECT?
DO YOU KNOW WHO GAVE ME THIS, SIR MORDRED?
NO, MY KING. I HAVE NOT SEEN IT BEFORE.
NO, I SUPPOSE YOU HAVEN'T.
IT WAS A GIFT FROM SOMEONE VERY CLOSE TO ME.
IT WAS A GIFT FROM SIR LEODEGRANCE. DID YOU KNOW HIM?
NO, MY LIEGE. HE WAS NOT HERE WHEN I JOINED YOUR KNIGHTS.
HE WAS MY QUEEN'S FATHER. HE GAVE ME THIS SOON AFTER I MARRIED GUINIVERE, ON THE OCCASION OF A TOURNAMENT I COMPETED IN.
IF I HOLD SIR LANCELOT TO THE RULE, THEN–
I MUST HOLD MY *WIFE* TO IT AS WELL.

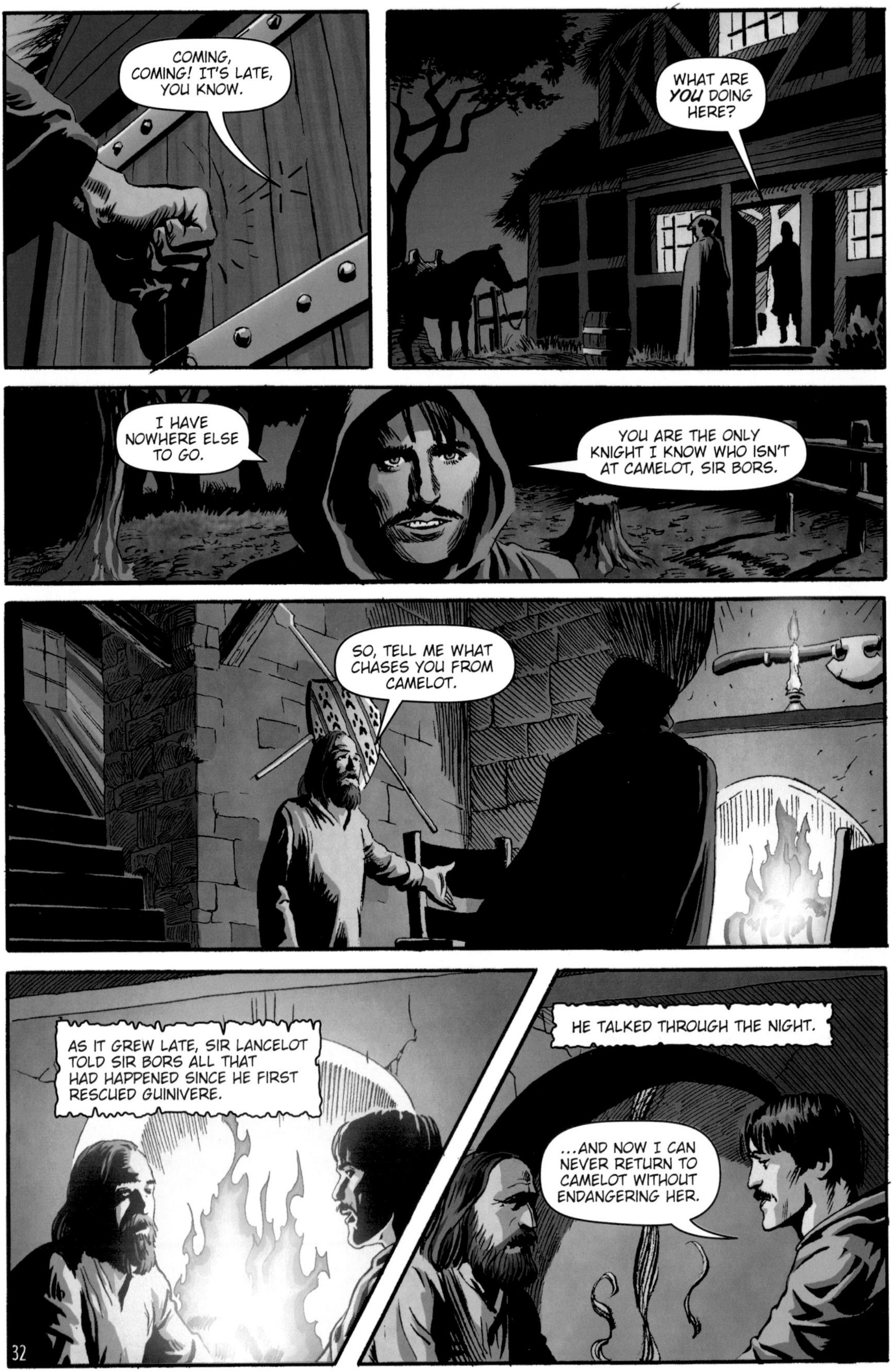

COMING, COMING! IT'S LATE, YOU KNOW.
WHAT ARE YOU DOING HERE?
I HAVE NOWHERE ELSE TO GO.
YOU ARE THE ONLY KNIGHT I KNOW WHO ISN'T AT CAMELOT, SIR BORS.
SO, TELL ME WHAT CHASES YOU FROM CAMELOT.
AS IT GREW LATE, SIR LANCELOT TOLD SIR BORS ALL THAT HAD HAPPENED SINCE HE FIRST RESCUED GUINIVERE.
HE TALKED THROUGH THE NIGHT.
...AND NOW I CAN NEVER RETURN TO CAMELOT WITHOUT ENDANGERING HER.

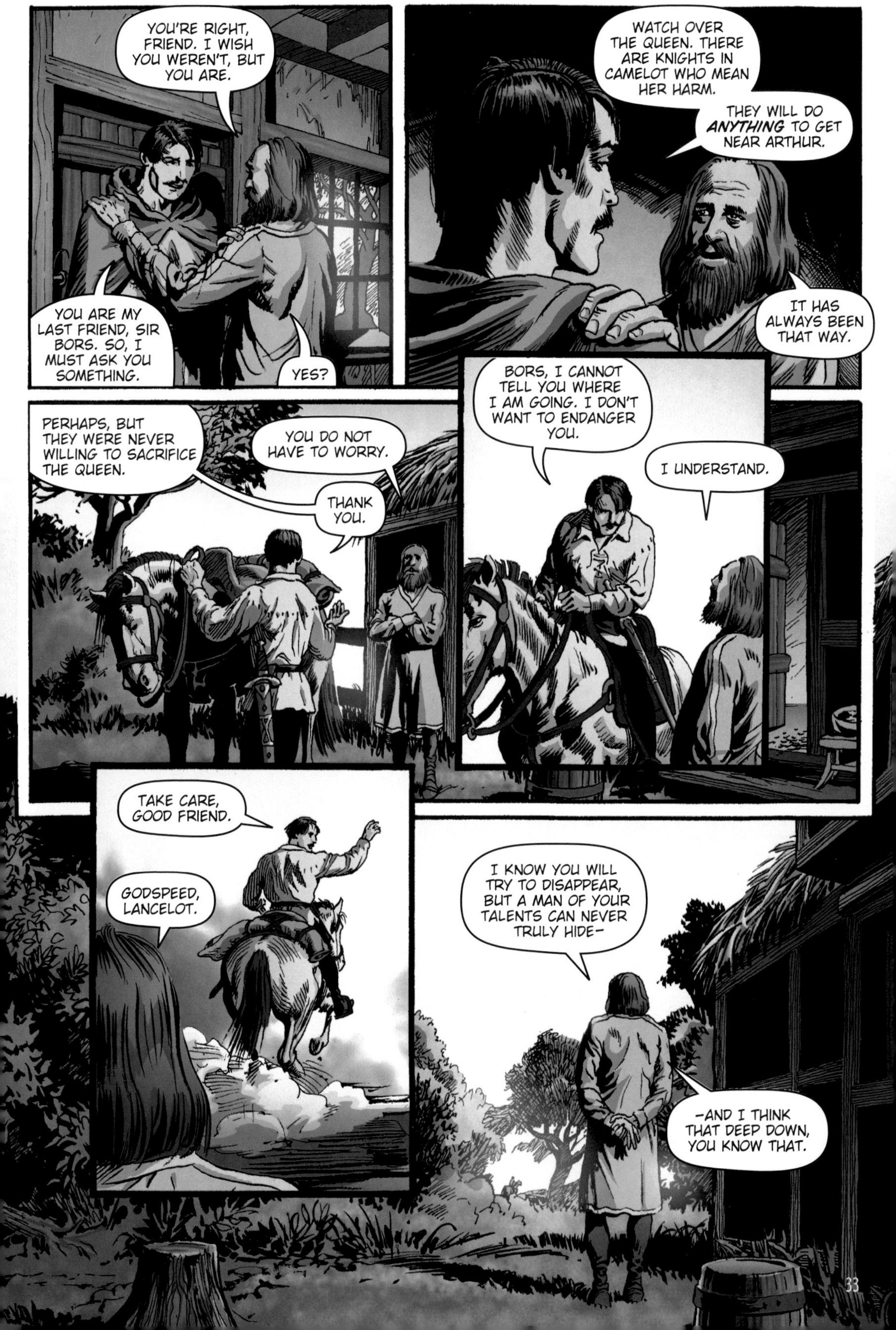
YOU'RE RIGHT, FRIEND. I WISH YOU WEREN'T, BUT YOU ARE.
YOU ARE MY LAST FRIEND, SIR BORS. SO, I MUST ASK YOU SOMETHING.
YES?
WATCH OVER THE QUEEN. THERE ARE KNIGHTS IN CAMELOT WHO MEAN HER HARM.
THEY WILL DO **ANYTHING** TO GET NEAR ARTHUR.
IT HAS ALWAYS BEEN THAT WAY.
PERHAPS, BUT THEY WERE NEVER WILLING TO SACRIFICE THE QUEEN.
YOU DO NOT HAVE TO WORRY.
THANK YOU.
BORS, I CANNOT TELL YOU WHERE I AM GOING. I DON'T WANT TO ENDANGER YOU.
I UNDERSTAND.
TAKE CARE, GOOD FRIEND.
GODSPEED, LANCELOT.
I KNOW YOU WILL TRY TO DISAPPEAR, BUT A MAN OF YOUR TALENTS CAN NEVER TRULY HIDE-
-AND I THINK THAT DEEP DOWN, YOU KNOW THAT.

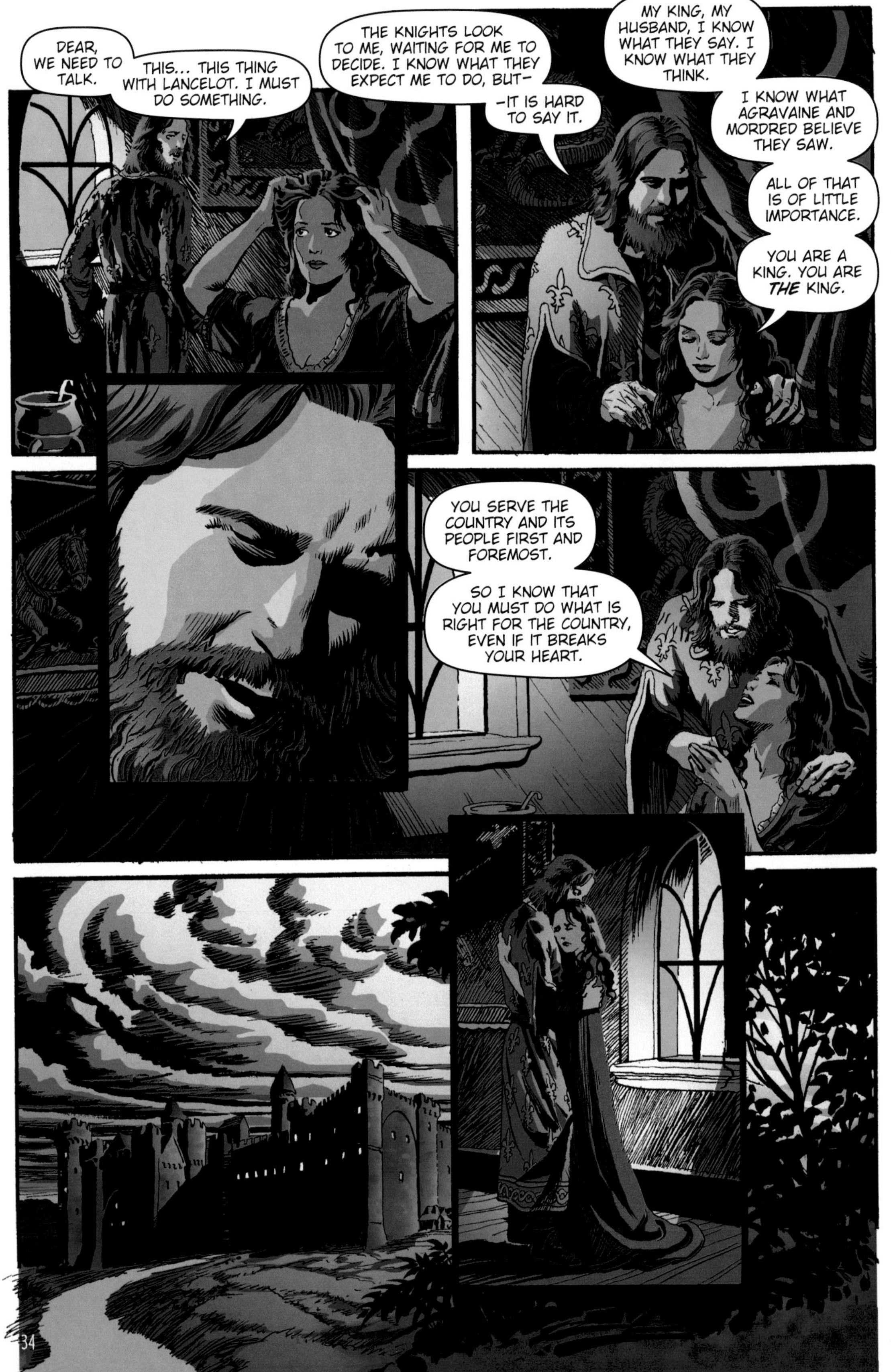
DEAR, WE NEED TO TALK.
THIS... THIS THING WITH LANCELOT. I MUST DO SOMETHING.
THE KNIGHTS LOOK TO ME, WAITING FOR ME TO DECIDE. I KNOW WHAT THEY EXPECT ME TO DO, BUT—
—IT IS HARD TO SAY IT.
MY KING, MY HUSBAND, I KNOW WHAT THEY SAY. I KNOW WHAT THEY THINK.
I KNOW WHAT AGRAVAINE AND MORDRED BELIEVE THEY SAW.
ALL OF THAT IS OF LITTLE IMPORTANCE.
YOU ARE A KING. YOU ARE *THE* KING.
YOU SERVE THE COUNTRY AND ITS PEOPLE FIRST AND FOREMOST.
SO I KNOW THAT YOU MUST DO WHAT IS RIGHT FOR THE COUNTRY, EVEN IF IT BREAKS YOUR HEART.

THE KNIGHTS OF THE ROUND TABLE TOOK TO THEIR HORSES, CROSSING ENGLAND IN SEARCH OF SIR LANCELOT.

BUT NO ONE COULD FIND THE FAMOUS KNIGHT.

IT WAS AS THOUGH HE HAD DISAPPEARED INTO THIN AIR.

SOME RUMORS SAID HE WAS DEAD OR INJURED AGAIN. OTHERS SAID HE HAD LEFT ENGLAND FOR HIS CASTLE IN FRANCE.

ONE KNIGHT KNEW THIS WASN'T TRUE.

SIR BORS HAD WATCHED OVER THE QUEEN WHILE LANCELOT WAS GONE, AS HE HAD PROMISED.

BUT HE KNEW HIS DUTY TO HIS KING CONFLICTED WITH HIS DUTY TO HIS FRIEND.

SO BORS SWORE TO HIMSELF THAT IF ANYONE WAS TO BRING IN LANCELOT, IT WOULD BE HE.

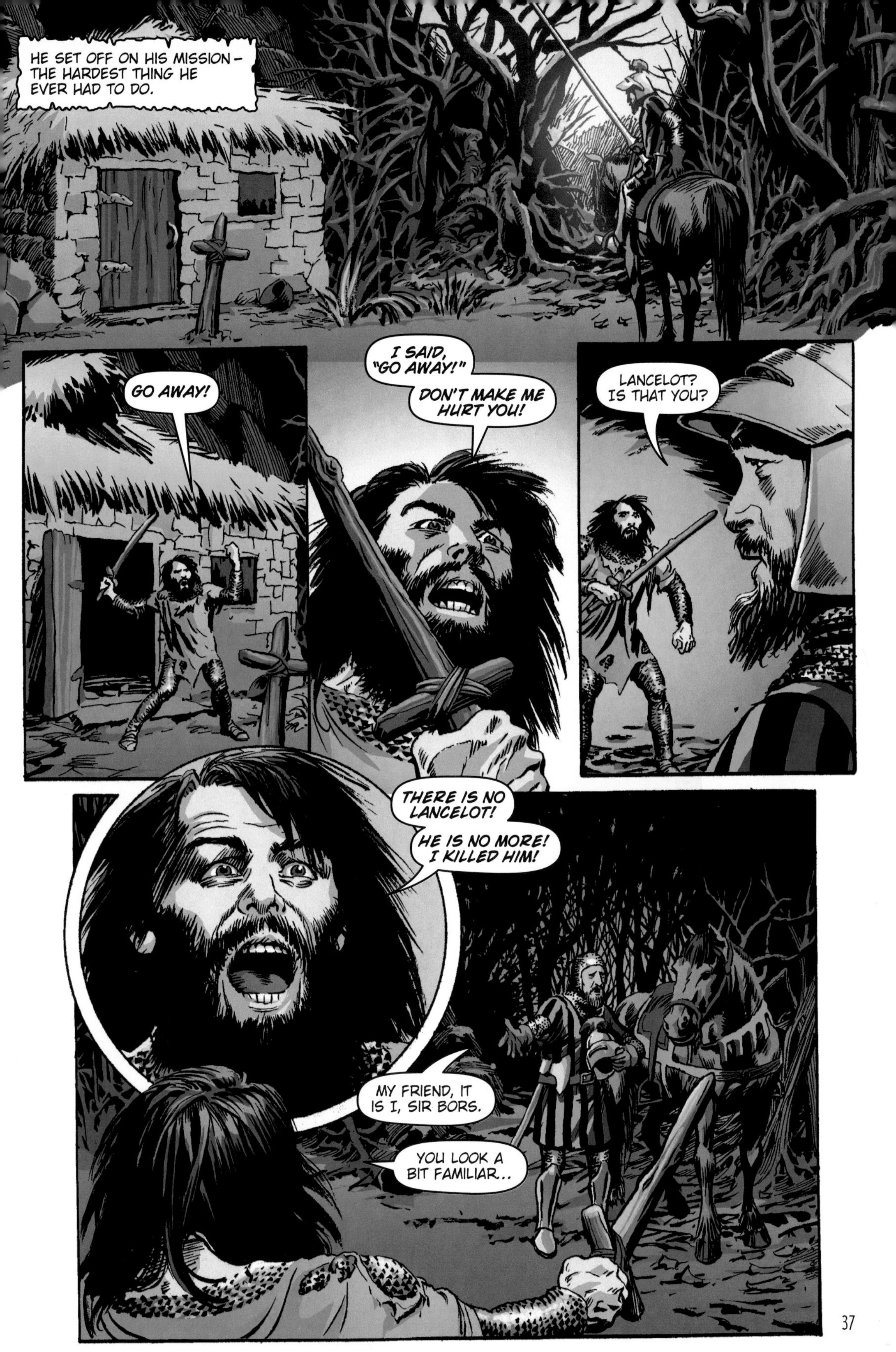
HE SET OFF ON HIS MISSION – THE HARDEST THING HE EVER HAD TO DO.
GO AWAY!
I SAID, "GO AWAY!"
DON'T MAKE ME HURT YOU!
LANCELOT? IS THAT YOU?
THERE IS NO LANCELOT!
HE IS NO MORE! I KILLED HIM!
MY FRIEND, IT IS I, SIR BORS.
YOU LOOK A BIT FAMILIAR...

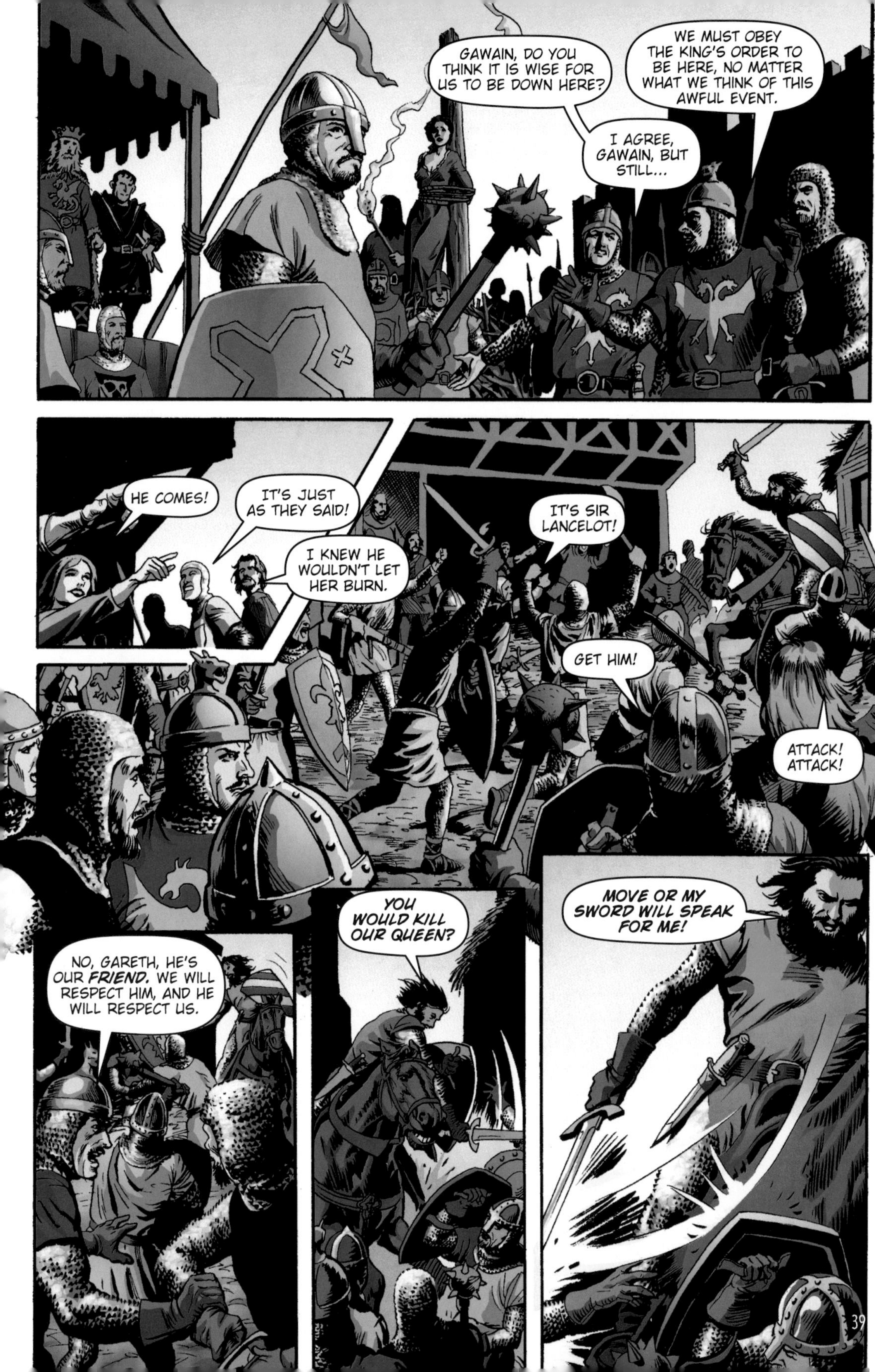
GAWAIN, DO YOU THINK IT IS WISE FOR US TO BE DOWN HERE?
WE MUST OBEY THE KING'S ORDER TO BE HERE, NO MATTER WHAT WE THINK OF THIS AWFUL EVENT.
I AGREE, GAWAIN, BUT STILL...
HE COMES!
IT'S JUST AS THEY SAID!
I KNEW HE WOULDN'T LET HER BURN.
IT'S SIR LANCELOT!
GET HIM!
ATTACK! ATTACK!
NO, GARETH, HE'S OUR *FRIEND.* WE WILL RESPECT HIM, AND HE WILL RESPECT US.
YOU WOULD KILL OUR QUEEN?
MOVE OR MY SWORD WILL SPEAK FOR ME!

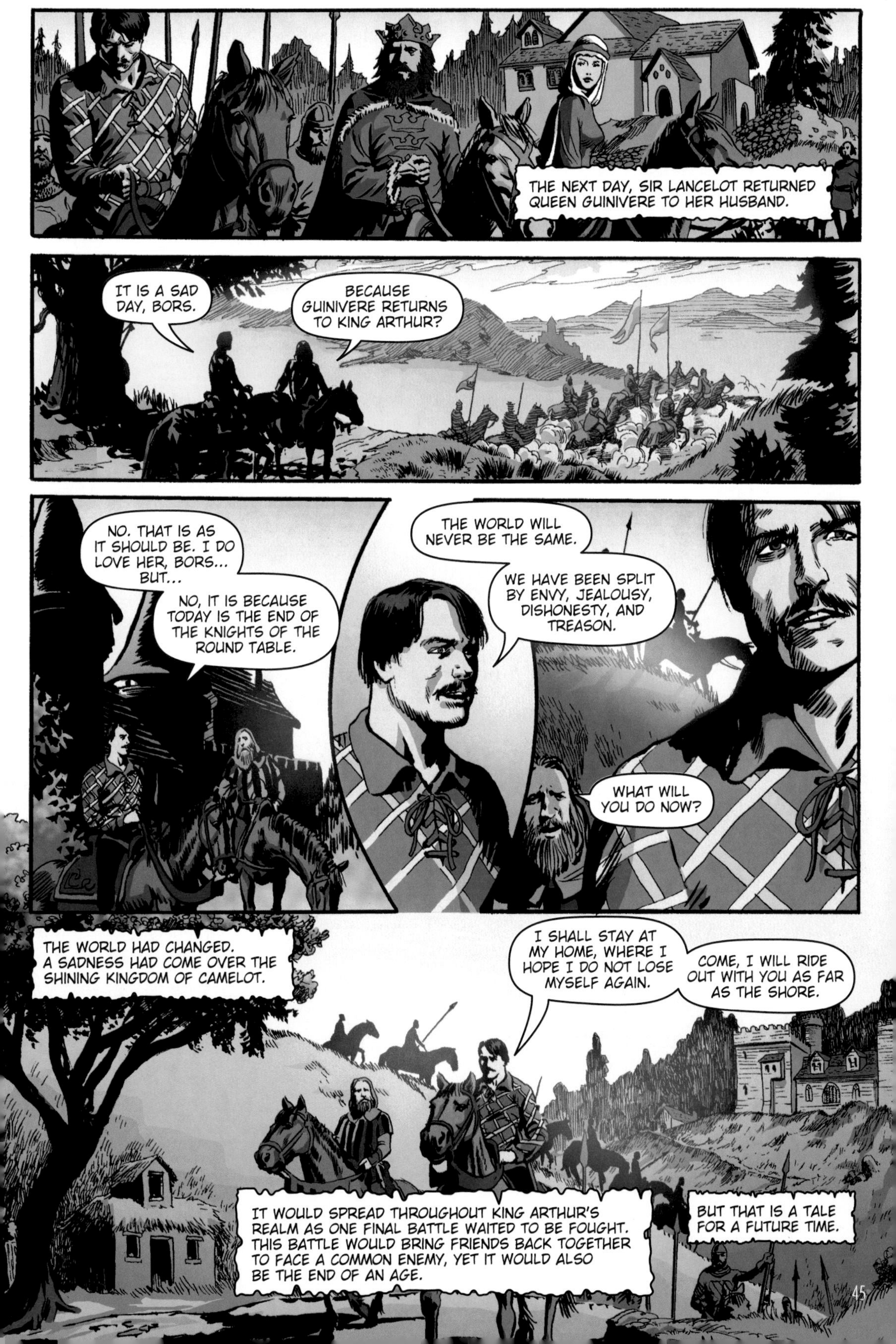
THE NEXT DAY, SIR LANCELOT RETURNED QUEEN GUINIVERE TO HER HUSBAND.
IT IS A SAD DAY, BORS.
BECAUSE GUINIVERE RETURNS TO KING ARTHUR?
NO. THAT IS AS IT SHOULD BE. I DO LOVE HER, BORS... BUT...
NO, IT IS BECAUSE TODAY IS THE END OF THE KNIGHTS OF THE ROUND TABLE.
THE WORLD WILL NEVER BE THE SAME.
WE HAVE BEEN SPLIT BY ENVY, JEALOUSY, DISHONESTY, AND TREASON.
WHAT WILL YOU DO NOW?
THE WORLD HAD CHANGED. A SADNESS HAD COME OVER THE SHINING KINGDOM OF CAMELOT.
I SHALL STAY AT MY HOME, WHERE I HOPE I DO NOT LOSE MYSELF AGAIN.
COME, I WILL RIDE OUT WITH YOU AS FAR AS THE SHORE.
IT WOULD SPREAD THROUGHOUT KING ARTHUR'S REALM AS ONE FINAL BATTLE WAITED TO BE FOUGHT. THIS BATTLE WOULD BRING FRIENDS BACK TOGETHER TO FACE A COMMON ENEMY, YET IT WOULD ALSO BE THE END OF AN AGE.
BUT THAT IS A TALE FOR A FUTURE TIME.

GLOSSARY AND PRONUNCIATION GUIDE

ARMOR: metal pieces once worn by soldiers to protect them from knife and arrow wounds

BOON: a favor given in answer to a request

CAMELOT: a castle and surrounding town that served as the capital of Arthur's kingdom

CHIVALRY: a code of behavior upheld by knights in the Middle Ages. Chivalrous knights vowed to obey religious law, defend the weak, serve their king, and protect their country.

COLORS: specific colors worn by knights and nobility in tournaments and battles. In chivalric tournaments, ladies also gave their colors to favored knights as a token of admiration.

GAWAIN (gah-*wayn*): one of the Knights of the Round Table

GUINIVERE (*gwen*-uh-veer): King Arthur's wife

HELM: a metal helmet worn with armor. Helms usually had a facepiece that could be moved up and down.

JOUST: a battle on horseback between two knights or among a group of knights. Jousts were often mock battles fought in tournaments. The purpose was merely to knock an opponent out of the saddle, but tournament jousts often resulted in real injuries.

KNIGHT: a mounted soldier sworn to loyally serve a lord or ruler

LANCELOT (*lan*-suh-laht): a French nobleman and one of the Knights of the Round Table

LIEGE: a superior, such as a lord or king, to whom others owe loyalty

LORD: a ruler or landowner with authority over a group of people

ROUND TABLE: a table given to King Arthur by his father-in-law, Leodegrance. Arthur's greatest knights were all given sieges, or special seats, at the Round Table.

SECOND: a knight or other combatant who assists someone in a one-on-one battle

TOURNAMENT: a series of jousts or sporting battles fought at one time and place

TRIAL BY MIGHT: a one-on-one battle used to settle disputes, also called a trial by combat. In the days before England had a regular court system, there were few ways of trying people accused of breaking the law or injuring someone else's rights. To settle certain issues, kings and local rulers allowed trials by might among anyone allowed to bear arms (that is, knights and nobility).

FURTHER READING AND WEBSITES

Camelot Village: Britain's Heritage and History
http://www.camelotintl.com/legend/index.html
This website provides basic information on Arthurian legends, with links to specific characters and to information on life in medieval England.

Crossley-Holland, Kevin. *The World of King Arthur and His Court: People, Places, Legend and Lore.* New York: Dutton Books, 2004. An illustrated guide providing information on key characters, daily life in a castle, knighthood, and other aspects of Arthurian legend.

King Arthur and the Knights of the Round Table
http://www.kingarthursknights.com
This website provides articles on the historical and legendary Arthur, a map and information on Arthurian sites, artwork, and the stories of the knights and other characters of the famous legend.

Limke, Jeff. *King Arthur: Excalibur Unsheathed.* Illustrated by Thomas Yeates. Minneapolis: Graphic Universe, 2007. This graphic novel begins as young Arthur pulls a mysterious sword from a stone and finds himself, at the age of ten, crowned the king of England. The magician Merlin guides Arthur in his efforts to win peace for his realm.

Roberts, Jeremy. *King Arthur.* Minneapolis: Twenty-First Century Books, 2001. This book examines both the historical and the literary Arthur, showing how he became a legendary hero.

CREATING *ARTHUR & LANCELOT: THE FIGHT FOR CAMELOT*

In creating the story, author Jeff Limke adapted *Le Morte d'Arthur*, written about 1485 by Sir Thomas Malory, an English knight. Artist Thomas Yeates used historical and traditional sources to shape the story's visual details. Consultant Andrew Scheil used his knowledge of Arthurian lore and medieval culture to ensure accuracy.

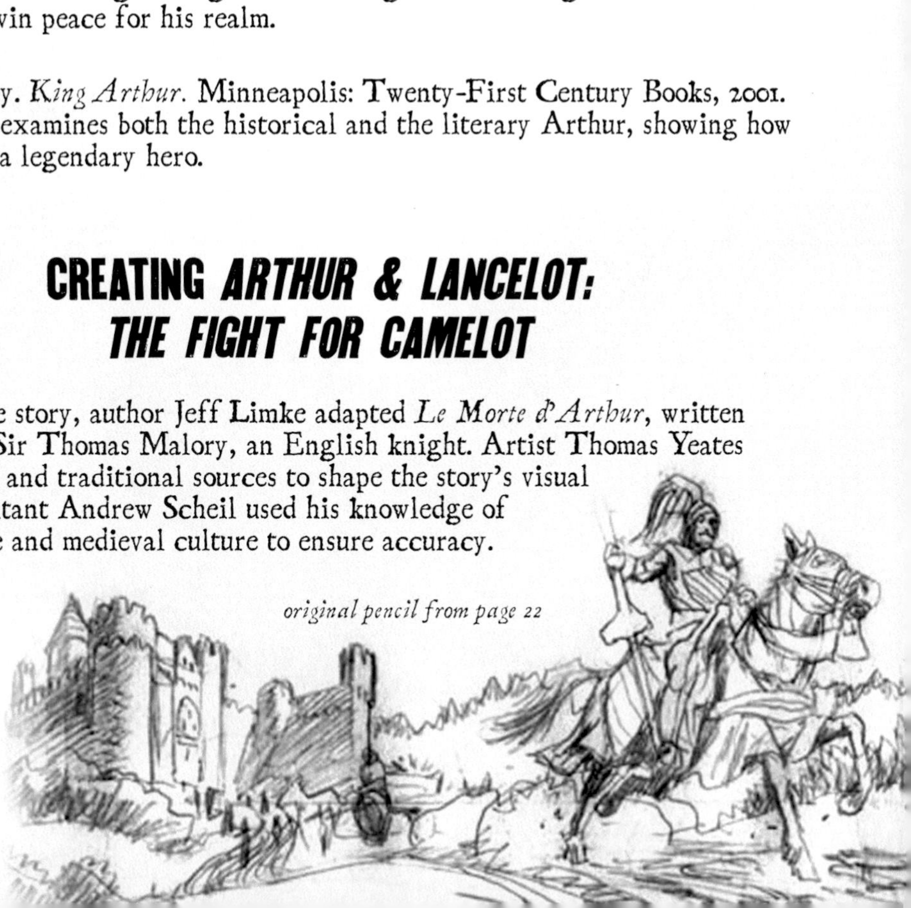

original pencil from page 22

INDEX

ABOUT THE AUTHOR AND THE ARTIST

JEFF LIMKE was raised in North Dakota, where he first read, listened to, and marveled at Arthurian tales of knights and their adventures. Limke later taught these stories for many years and has written several adaptations of them. His Graphic Myths and Legends work includes *King Arthur: Excalibur Unsheathed*, *Isis & Osiris: To the Ends of the Earth*, *Thor & Loki: In the Land of Giants*, *Jason: Quest for the Golden Fleece*, and *Theseus: Battling the Minotaur*. Other stories have been published by Caliber Comics, Arrow Comics, and Kenzer and Company.

THOMAS YEATES began his art training in high school and continued at Utah State University and Sacramento State. Subsequently, he was a member of the first class at Joe Kubert's School, a trade program for aspiring comic book artists in New Jersey. Yeates has worked as an illustrator for DC Comics, Marvel, Dark Horse, and many other companies, drawing Tarzan, Zorro, the Swamp Thing, Timespirits, Captain America, and Conan. For Graphic Myths and Legends, he has illustrated *King Arthur: Excalibur Unsheathed*, *Robin Hood: Outlaw of Sherwood Forest*, *Atalanta: Race Against Destiny*, and *Odysseus: Escaping Poseidon's Curse*. Yeates lives in northern California with his wife and daughter.